# The 46 Basic Hiragana Characters

The chart below shows the 46 basic characters in the hiragana alphabet with their pronunciation. Hiragana is generally used for grammatical endings and words that don't have kanji.

| | | | | |
|---|---|---|---|---|
| あ<br>**a** | い<br>**i** | う<br>**u** | え<br>**e** | |
| か<br>**ka** | き<br>**ki** | く<br>**ku** | け<br>**ke** | こ<br>**ko** |
| さ<br>**sa** | し<br>**shi** | す<br>**su** | せ<br>**se** | そ<br>**so** |
| た<br>**ta** | ち<br>**chi** | つ<br>**tsu** | て<br>**te** | と<br>**to** |
| な<br>**na** | に<br>**ni** | ぬ<br>**nu** | ね<br>**ne** | の<br>**no** |
| は<br>**ha (wa)** | ひ<br>**hi** | ふ<br>**fu** | へ<br>**he (e)** | ほ<br>**ho** |
| ま<br>**ma** | み<br>**mi** | む<br>**mu** | め<br>**me** | も<br>**mo** |
| や<br>**ya** | | ゆ<br>**yu** | | よ<br>**yo** |
| ら<br>**ra** | り<br>**ri** | る<br>**ru** | れ<br>**re** | ろ<br>**ro** |
| わ<br>**wa** | | | | を<br>**w(o)** |
| ん<br>**n** | | | | |

# 🎧 The 61 Additional Hiragana Characters

Adding two small lines to a hiragana syllable makes the sound hard. *Ka* becomes *ga*, *sa* becomes *za*, etc. Adding a small circle to the syllables starting with *h* makes a *p* sound. In the lower two tables the *i*-column syllable combines with *ya*, *yu* or *yo* to make the sounds *kya*, *kyu*, *kyo*, etc.

| | | | | |
|---|---|---|---|---|
| が<br>ga | ぎ<br>gi | ぐ<br>gu | げ<br>ge | ご<br>go |
| ざ<br>za | じ<br>ji | ず<br>zu | ぜ<br>ze | ぞ<br>zo |
| だ<br>da | ぢ<br>ji | づ<br>zu | で<br>de | ど<br>do |
| ば<br>ba | び<br>bi | ぶ<br>bu | べ<br>be | ぼ<br>bo |
| ぱ<br>pa | ぴ<br>pi | ぷ<br>pu | ぺ<br>pe | ぽ<br>po |

| | | | | | |
|---|---|---|---|---|---|
| きゃ<br>kya | きゅ<br>kyu | きょ<br>kyo | じゃ<br>ja | じゅ<br>ju | じょ<br>jo |
| しゃ<br>sha | しゅ<br>shu | しょ<br>sho | ぢゃ<br>ja | ぢゅ<br>ju | ぢょ<br>jo |
| ちゃ<br>cha | ちゅ<br>chu | ちょ<br>cho | みゃ<br>mya | みゅ<br>myu | みょ<br>myo |
| にゃ<br>nya | にゅ<br>nyu | にょ<br>nyo | りゃ<br>rya | りゅ<br>ryu | りょ<br>ryo |
| ひゃ<br>hya | ひゅ<br>hyu | ひょ<br>hyo | びゃ<br>bya | びゅ<br>byu | びょ<br>byo |
| ぎゃ<br>gya | ぎゅ<br>gyu | ぎょ<br>gyo | ぴゃ<br>pya | ぴゅ<br>pyu | ぴょ<br>pyo |

## 🎧 The 46 Basic Katakana Characters

The chart below shows the 46 basic characters in the katakana alphabet with their pronunciation. Katakana is used for writing foreign loan words, for emphasis and for onomatopoeia.

| | | | | |
|---|---|---|---|---|
| ア **a** | イ **i** | ウ **u** | エ **e** | オ **o** |
| カ **ka** | キ **ki** | ク **ku** | ケ **ke** | コ **ko** |
| サ **sa** | シ **shi** | ス **su** | セ **se** | ソ **so** |
| タ **ta** | チ **chi** | ツ **tsu** | テ **te** | ト **to** |
| ナ **na** | ニ **ni** | ヌ **nu** | ネ **ne** | ノ **no** |
| ハ **ha/wa** | ヒ **hi** | フ **fu** | ヘ **h(e)** | ホ **ho** |
| マ **ma** | ミ **mi** | ム **mu** | メ **me** | モ **mo** |
| ヤ **ya** | | ユ **yu** | | ヨ **yo** |
| ラ **ra** | リ **ri** | ル **ru** | レ **re** | ロ **ro** |
| ワ **wa** | | | | ヲ **w(o)** |
| ン **n** | | | | |

# 🎧 The 50 Additional Katakana Characters

Adding two small lines to a katakana syllable makes the sound hard. *Ka* becomes *ga*, *sa* becomes *za*, etc. Adding a small circle to the syllables starting with *h* makes a *p* sound. In the lower two tables the *i*-column syllable combines with *ya*, *yu* or *yo* to make the sounds *kya*, *kyu*, *kyo*, etc.

| | | | | |
|---|---|---|---|---|
| ガ<br>**ga** | ギ<br>**gi** | グ<br>**gu** | ゲ<br>**ge** | ゴ<br>**go** |
| ザ<br>**za** | ジ<br>**ji** | ズ<br>**zu** | ゼ<br>**ze** | ゾ<br>**zo** |
| ダ<br>**da** | | | デ<br>**de** | ド<br>**do** |
| バ<br>**ba** | ビ<br>**bi** | ブ<br>**bu** | ベ<br>**be** | ボ<br>**bo** |
| パ<br>**pa** | ピ<br>**pi** | プ<br>**pu** | ペ<br>**pe** | ポ<br>**po** |

| | | |
|---|---|---|
| キャ<br>**kya** | キュ<br>**kyu** | キョ<br>**kyo** |
| シャ<br>**sha** | シュ<br>**shu** | ショ<br>**sho** |
| チャ<br>**cha** | チュ<br>**chu** | チョ<br>**cho** |
| ニャ<br>**nya** | ニュ<br>**nyu** | ニョ<br>**nyo** |
| ヒャ<br>**hya** | ヒュ<br>**hyu** | ヒョ<br>**hyo** |

| | | |
|---|---|---|
| ギャ<br>**gya** | ギュ<br>**gyu** | ギョ<br>**gyo** |
| ジャ<br>**ja** | ジュ<br>**ju** | ジョ<br>**jo** |
| ミャ<br>**mya** | ミュ<br>**myu** | ミョ<br>**myo** |
| リャ<br>**rya** | リュ<br>**ryu** | リョ<br>**ryo** |

# How to Write Hiragana and Katakana Characters

The strokes of hiragana and katakana are always written from left to right and from top to bottom. Each stroke will have one of the following types of ending: とめ **tome** (stop), はね **hane** (jump) or はらい **harai** (sweep). A stop is when the stroke comes to a stop before you move your pen from the paper. A jump is a small flourish made by removing the pen from the paper as you move to the next stroke. A sweep is when the pen is slowly removed from the end of the stroke in a sweeping motion. In the letter **ke** shown on the right, stroke 1 is a jump, stroke 2 is a stop and stroke 3 is a sweep.

## Hiragana Writing Practice
## The 46 Basic Characters with Stroke Orders

5

| su | すｰす | | | | | | | | | | | | |
|----|-------|--|--|--|--|--|--|--|--|--|--|--|--|
| se | せ ｰ ナ せ | | | | | | | | | | | | |
| so | そ そ | | | | | | | | | | | | |
| ta | た ｰ た た た | | | | | | | | | | | | |
| chi | ち ｰ ち | | | | | | | | | | | | |
| tsu | つ つ | | | | | | | | | | | | |
| te | て て | | | | | | | | | | | | |
| to | と と | | | | | | | | | | | | |
| na | な ｰ た た な | | | | | | | | | | | | |
| ni | に に に に | | | | | | | | | | | | |
| nu | ぬ ぬ ぬ | | | | | | | | | | | | |
| ne | ね ね ね | | | | | | | | | | | | |
| no | の の | | | | | | | | | | | | |
| ha | は に に は | | | | | | | | | | | | |
| hi | ひ ひ | | | | | | | | | | | | |
| fu | ふ ふ ふ ふ | | | | | | | | | | | | |
| he | へ へ | | | | | | | | | | | | |

| ho | ほ | | | | | | | | | | | |
| ma | ま | | | | | | | | | | | |
| mi | み | | | | | | | | | | | |
| mu | む | | | | | | | | | | | |
| me | め | | | | | | | | | | | |
| mo | も | | | | | | | | | | | |
| ya | や | | | | | | | | | | | |
| yu | ゆ | | | | | | | | | | | |
| yo | よ | | | | | | | | | | | |
| ra | ら | | | | | | | | | | | |
| ri | り | | | | | | | | | | | |
| ru | る | | | | | | | | | | | |
| re | れ | | | | | | | | | | | |
| ro | ろ | | | | | | | | | | | |
| wa | わ | | | | | | | | | | | |
| (w)o | を | | | | | | | | | | | |
| n | ん | | | | | | | | | | | |

# Katakana Writing Practice
## The 46 Basic Characters with Stroke Orders

| | | | | | | | | | | | | | |
|---|---|---|---|---|---|---|---|---|---|---|---|---|---|
| a ア | ラ | ア | | | | | | | | | | | |
| i イ | ソ | イ | | | | | | | | | | | |
| u ウ | ウ | セ | ウ | | | | | | | | | | |
| e エ | ー | エ | エ | | | | | | | | | | |
| o オ | ー | オ | オ | | | | | | | | | | |
| ka カ | フ | カ | | | | | | | | | | | |
| ki キ | ー | キ | キ | | | | | | | | | | |
| ku ク | ク | ク | | | | | | | | | | | |
| ke ケ | ソ | ケ | ケ | | | | | | | | | | |
| ko コ | コ | コ | | | | | | | | | | | |
| sa サ | ー | サ | サ | | | | | | | | | | |
| shi シ | シ | シ | シ | | | | | | | | | | |
| su ス | ス | ス | | | | | | | | | | | |
| se セ | セ | セ | | | | | | | | | | | |
| so ソ | ソ | ソ | | | | | | | | | | | |
| ta タ | タ | タ | タ | | | | | | | | | | |

8

| me | メ | ノ | メ | | | | | | | | | |
| mo | モ | ニ | ニ | モ | | | | | | | | |
| ya | ヤ | ウ | ヤ | | | | | | | | | |
| yu | ユ | フ | ユ | | | | | | | | | |
| yo | ヨ | フ | ヲ | ヨ | | | | | | | | |
| ra | ラ | ニ | ラ | | | | | | | | | |
| ri | リ | リ | リ | | | | | | | | | |
| ru | ル | ノ | ル | | | | | | | | | |
| re | レ | レ | | | | | | | | | | |
| ro | ロ | ロ | ロ | ロ | | | | | | | | |
| wa | ワ | ワ | ワ | | | | | | | | | |
| (w)o | ヲ | フ | ヲ | | | | | | | | | |
| n | ン | ン | ン | | | | | | | | | |

## 🎧 Handwriting Practice

The exercises on the following pages will help you practice writing the hiragana and katakana characters you have studied in a variety of useful, everyday words.

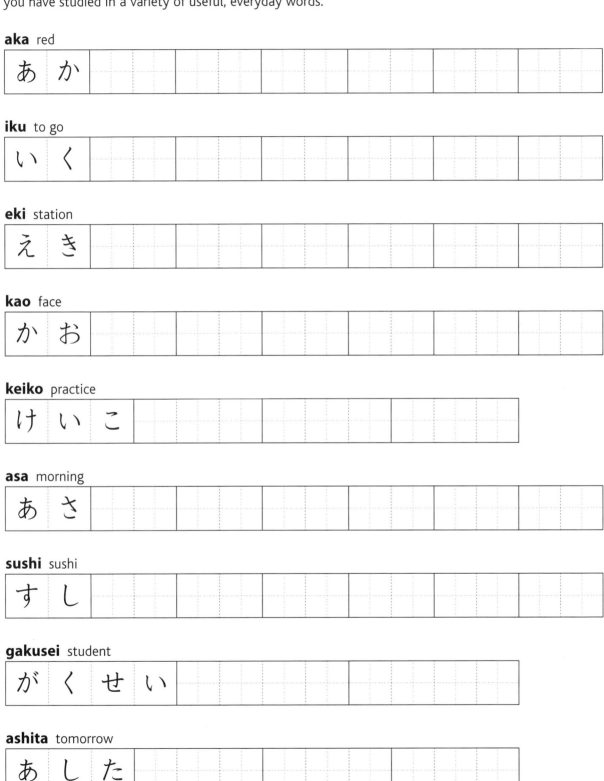

**aka** red

あ か

**iku** to go

い く

**eki** station

え き

**kao** face

か お

**keiko** practice

け い こ

**asa** morning

あ さ

**sushi** sushi

す し

**gakusei** student

が く せ い

**ashita** tomorrow

あ し た

**kazoku** family

かぞく

**chikatetsu** subway

ちかてつ

**shigoto** work

しごと

**nani** what

なに

**inu** dog

いぬ

**okane** money

おかね

**kimono** kimono

きもの

**hai** yes

はい

**hito** person

ひと

**fuyu** winter

ふゆ

**heta** bad at something

へ た

**hoshi** star

ほ し

**atama** head

あ た ま

**sashimi** sashimi

さ し み

**yomu** to read

よ む

**yume** dream

ゆ め

**oyasumi** good night

お や す み

**yubi** finger

ゆ び

**yōkoso** welcome

よ う こ そ

**karada** body

か ら だ

**onigiri** rice ball

おにぎり

**haru** spring

はる

**hiroi** wide

ひろい

**kore** this

これ

**watashi** I, me

わたし

**tenki** weather

てんき

**gakkō** school

がっこう

**gyūnyū** milk

ぎゅうにゅう

**soba** soba noodles

そば

**yappari** sure enough

やっぱり

**aisu** ice

| ア | イ | ス | | | | | | | | | | |

**hausu** house

| ハ | ウ | ス | | | | | | | | | | |

**eko** ecology

| エ | コ | | | | | | | |

**oranda** Holland

| オ | ラ | ン | ダ | | | | | | |

**kanada** Canada

| カ | ナ | ダ | | | | | | | | |

**kēki** cake

| ケ | ー | キ | | | | | | | | |

**haiteku** high tech

| ハ | イ | テ | ク | | | | | | |

**saizu** size

| サ | イ | ズ | | | | | | | | |

**shikago** Chicago

| シ | カ | ゴ | | | | | | | | |

**sukī** skiing

| ス | キ | ー | | | | | | | | |

**gasu** gas

ガ ス

**akusesu** access

ア ク セ ス

**sōsu** sauce

ソ ー ス

**takushī** taxi

タ ク シ ー

**chīzu** cheese

チ ー ズ

**shītsu** sheet

シ ー ツ

**tesuto** test

テ ス ト

**tenisu** tennis

テ ニ ス

**kanū** canoe

カ ヌ ー

**kone** connection

コ ネ

**nōto** note

ノ ー ト

**kōhī** coffee

コ ー ヒ ー

**naifu** knife

ナ イ フ

**bēbī** baby

ベ ー ビ ー

**hōmupēji** home page

ホ ー ム ペ ー ジ

**sumaho** smart phone

ス マ ホ

**masukomi** mass media

マ ス コ ミ

**mōru** mall

モ ー ル

**myūjikku** music

ミ ュ ー ジ ッ ク

**taiya** tire

タ イ ヤ

**yoga** yoga

ヨ ガ

**washinton** Washington

ワ シ ン ト ン

**rate** latte

ラ テ

**kurisumasu** Christmas

ク リ ス マ ス

**toire** toilet

ト イ レ

**yūro** euro

ユ ー ロ

**kyasshu** cash

キ ャ ッ シ ュ

**orinpikku** Olympics

オ リ ン ピ ッ ク

**vaiorin** violin

ヴ ァ イ オ リ ン

**shefu** chef

シ ェ フ

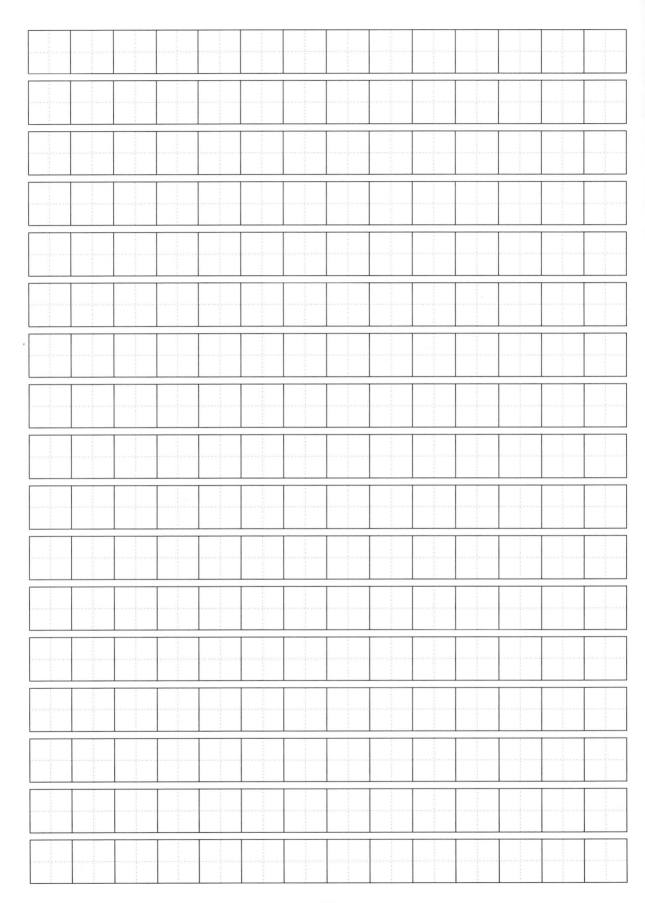

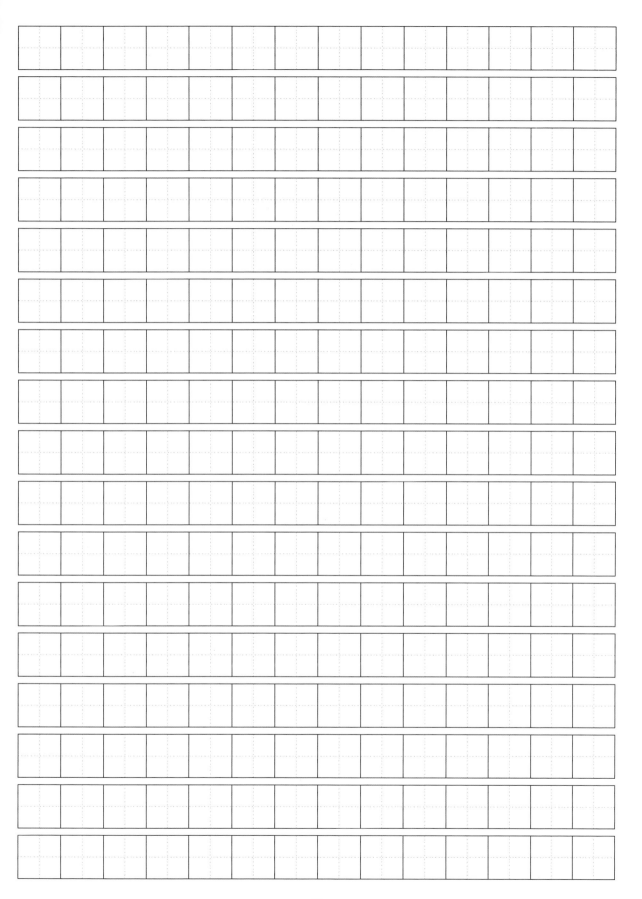

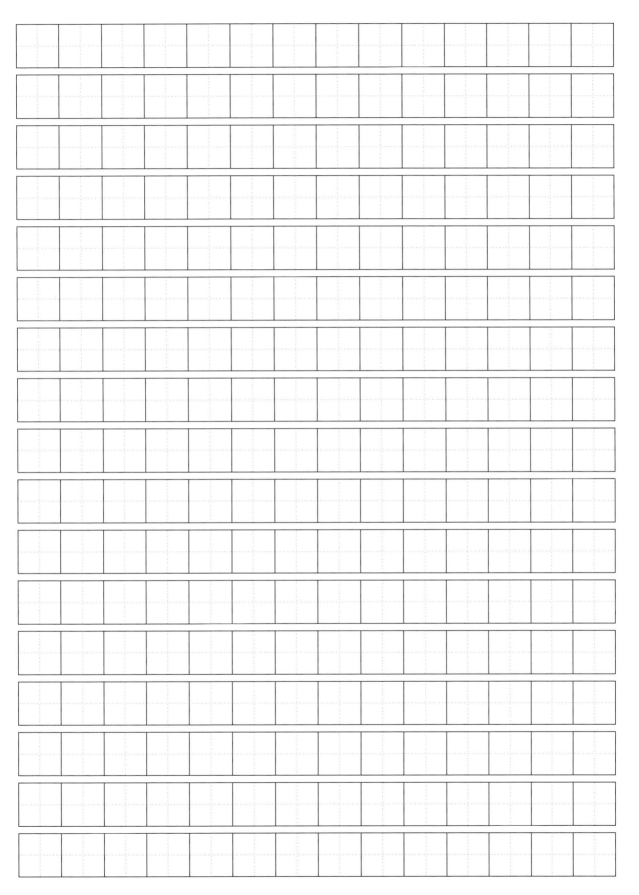

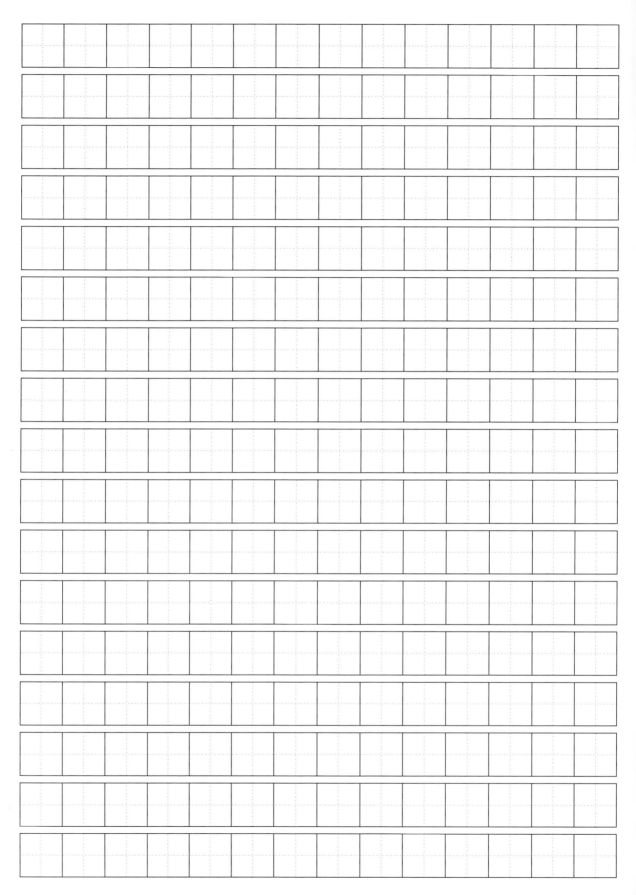

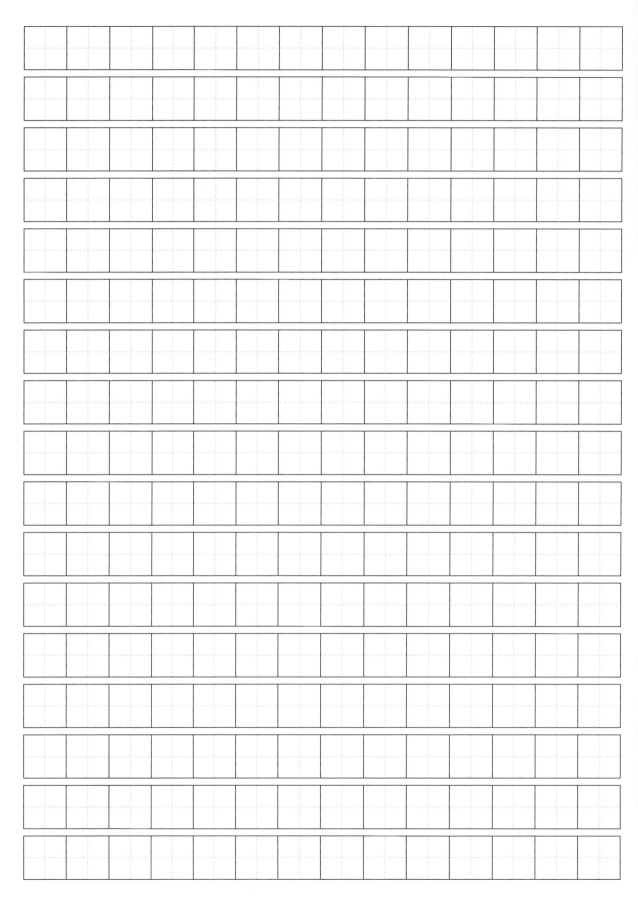

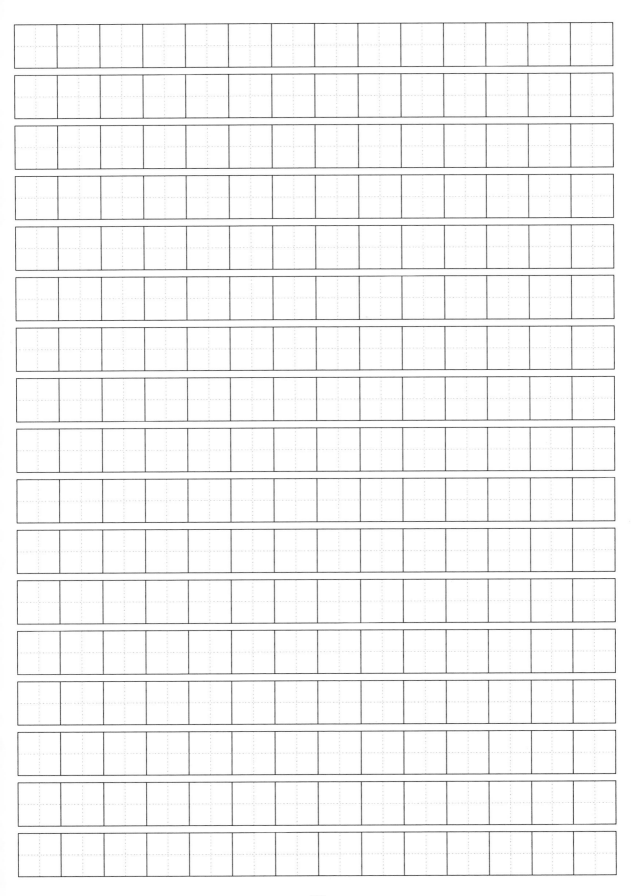

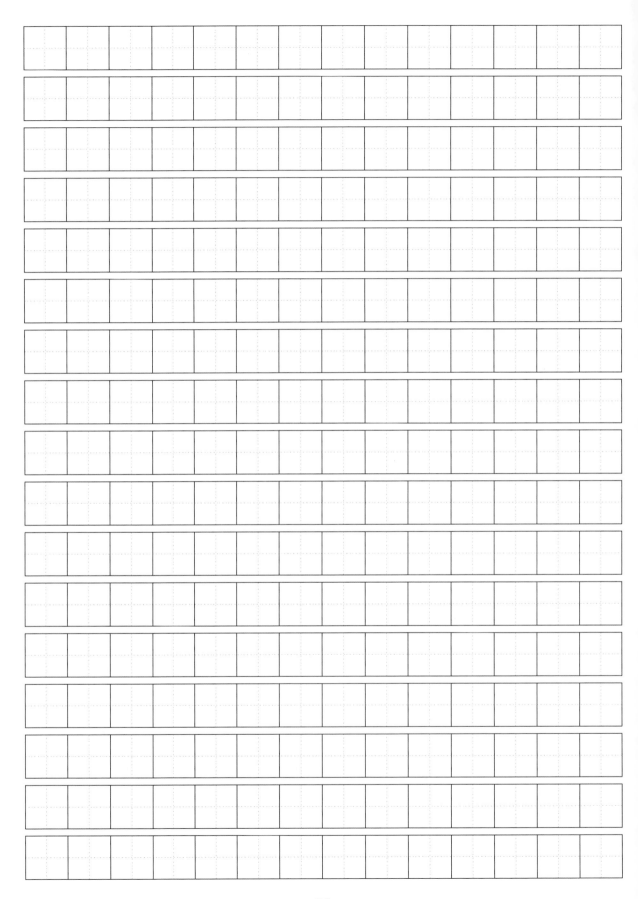

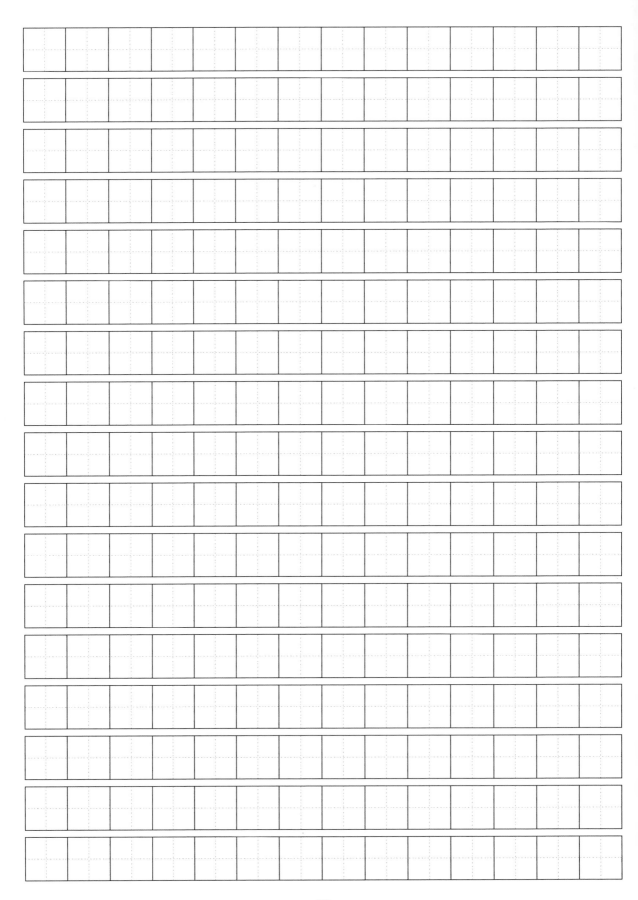

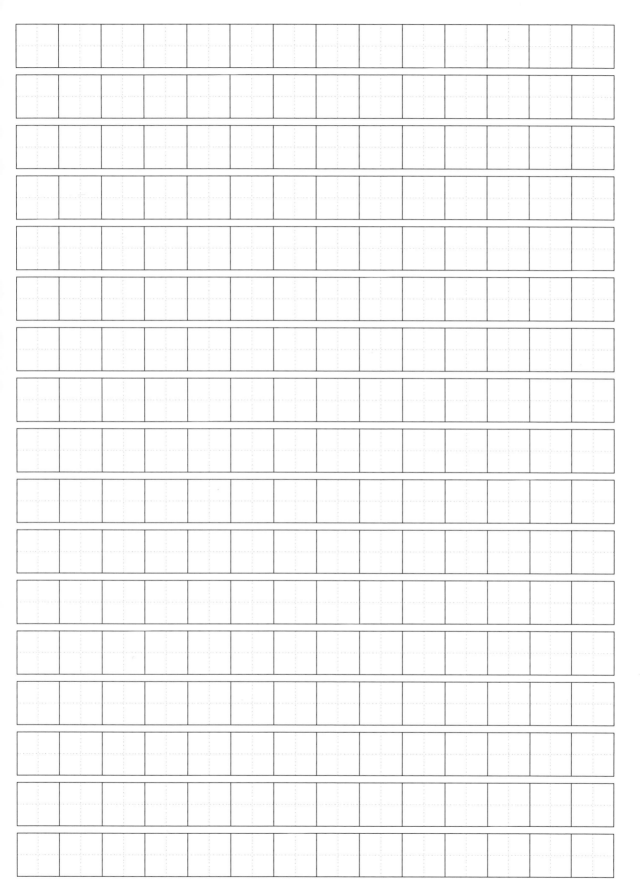

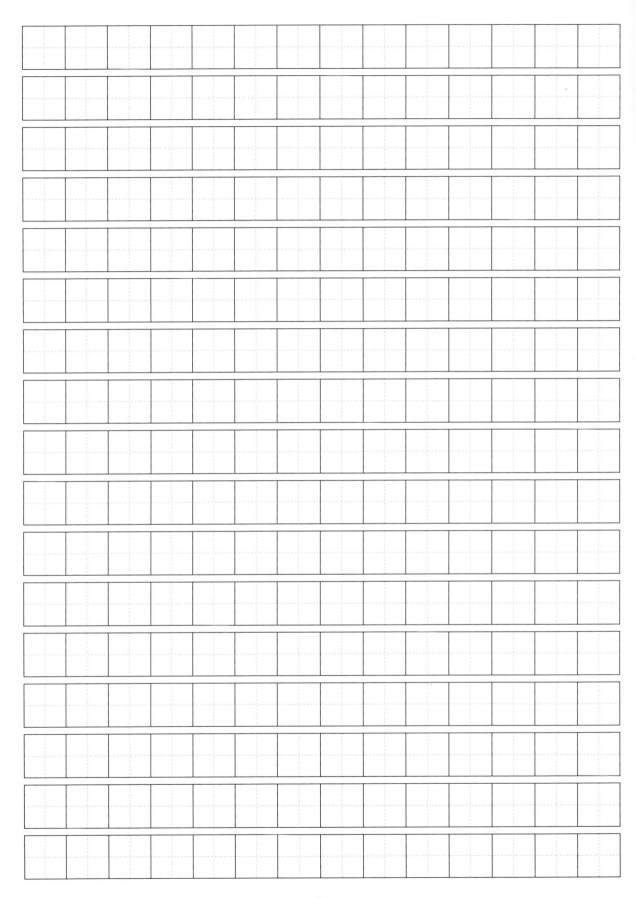

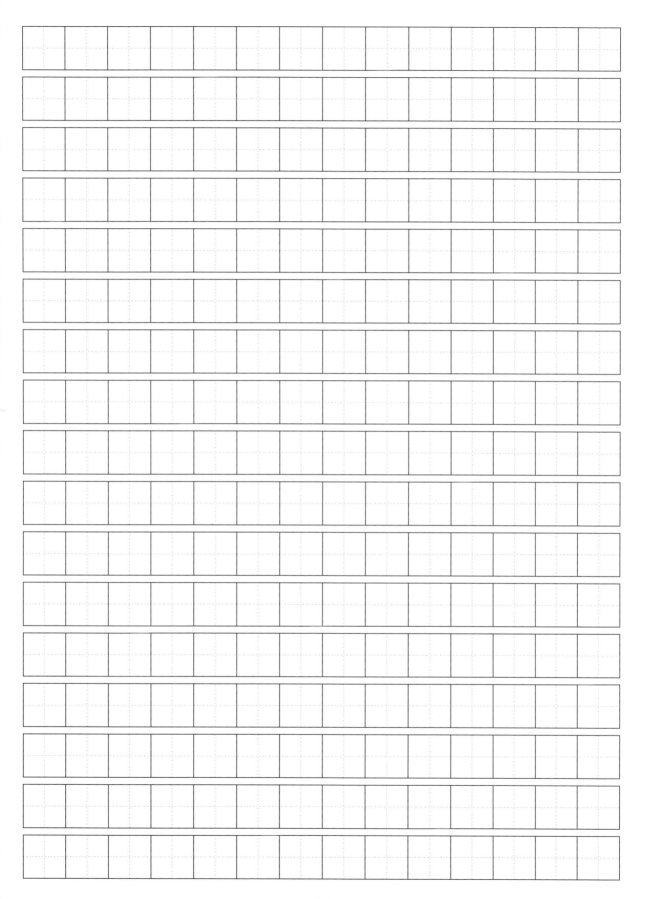

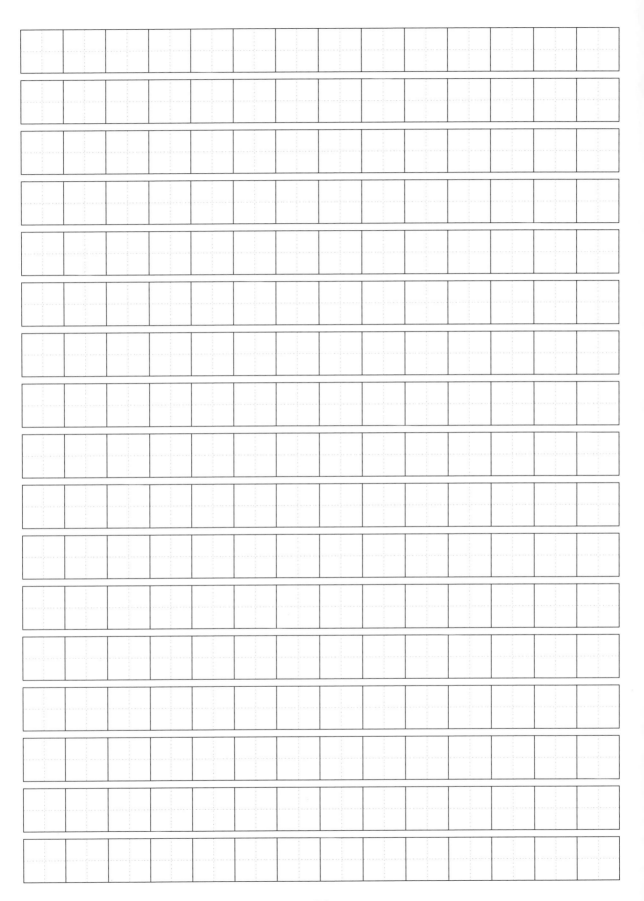

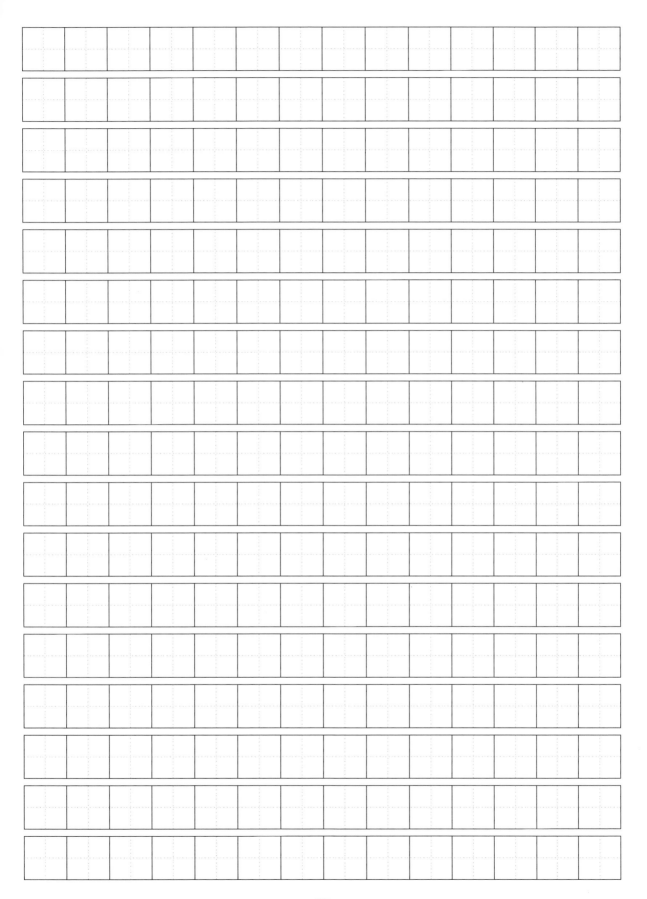

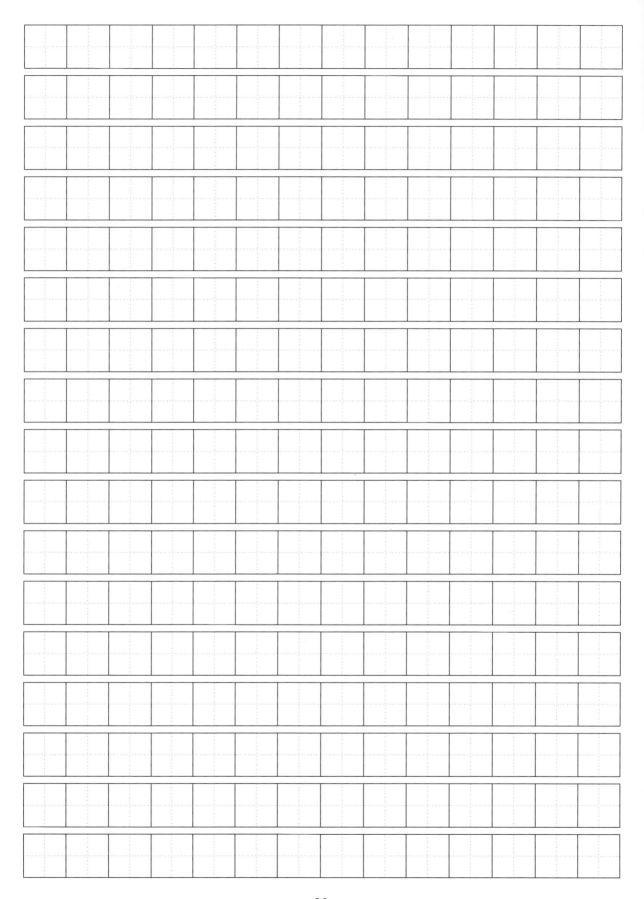

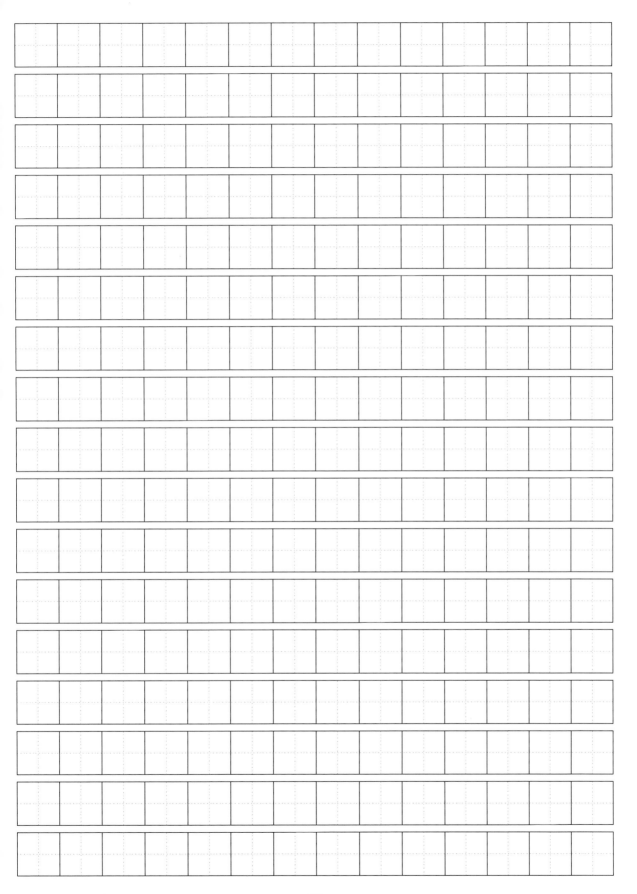

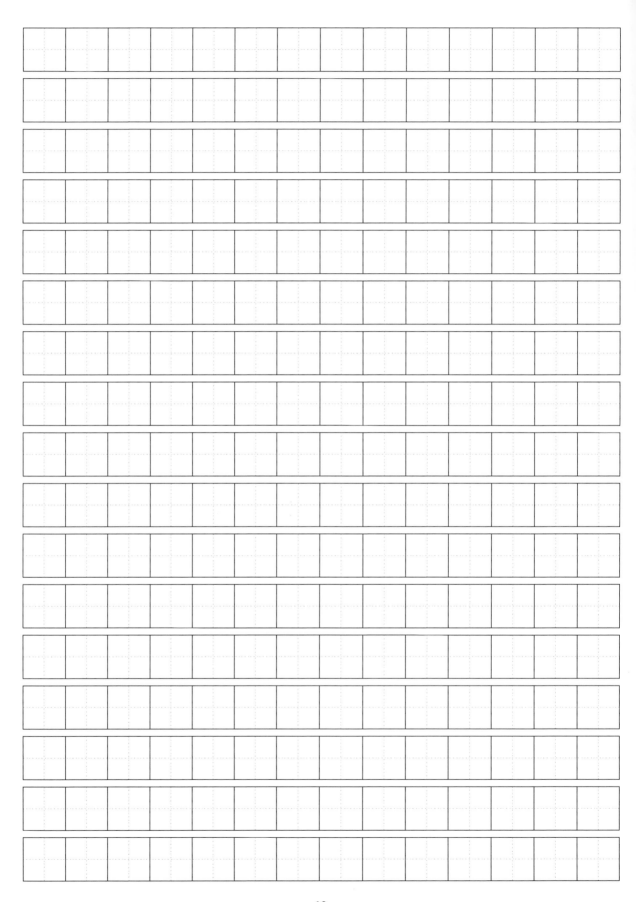

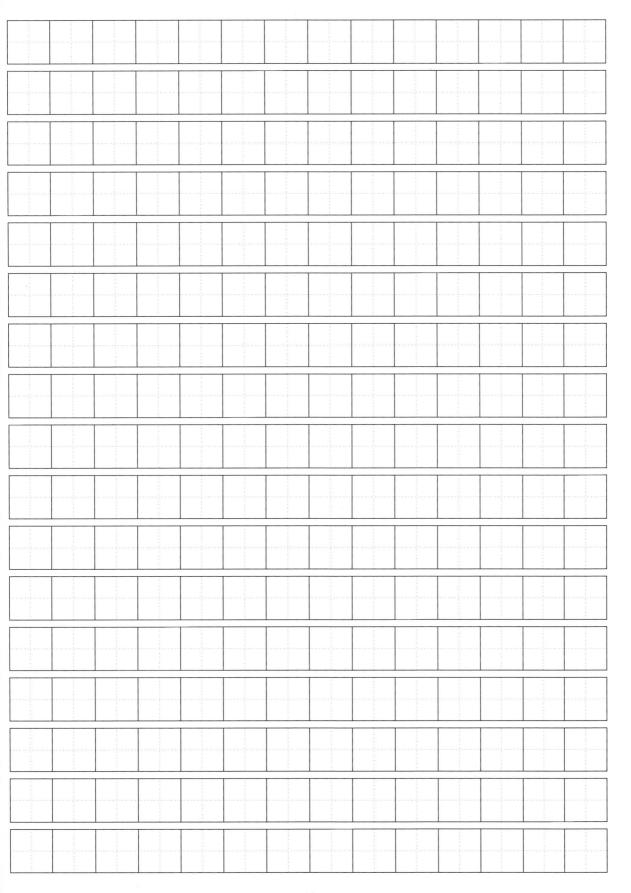

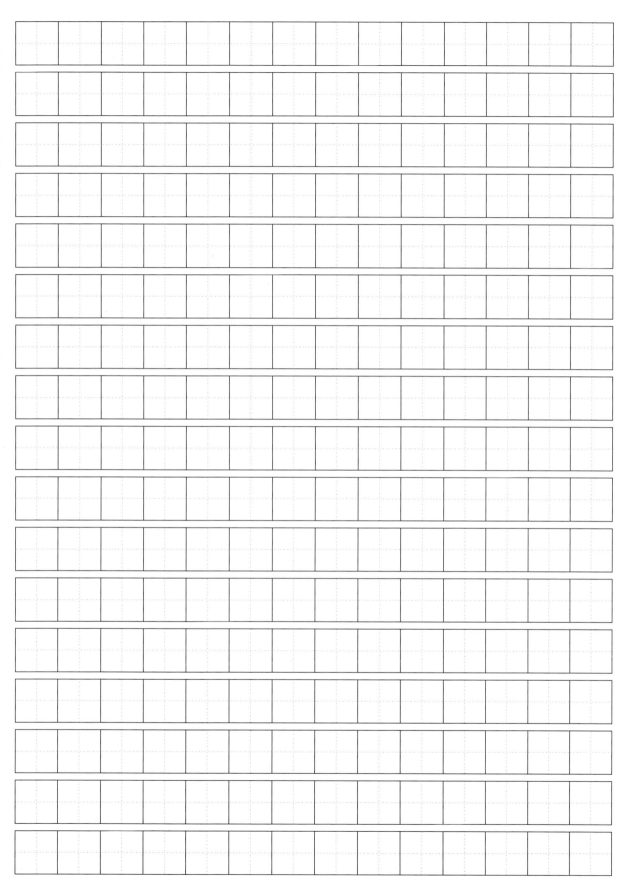

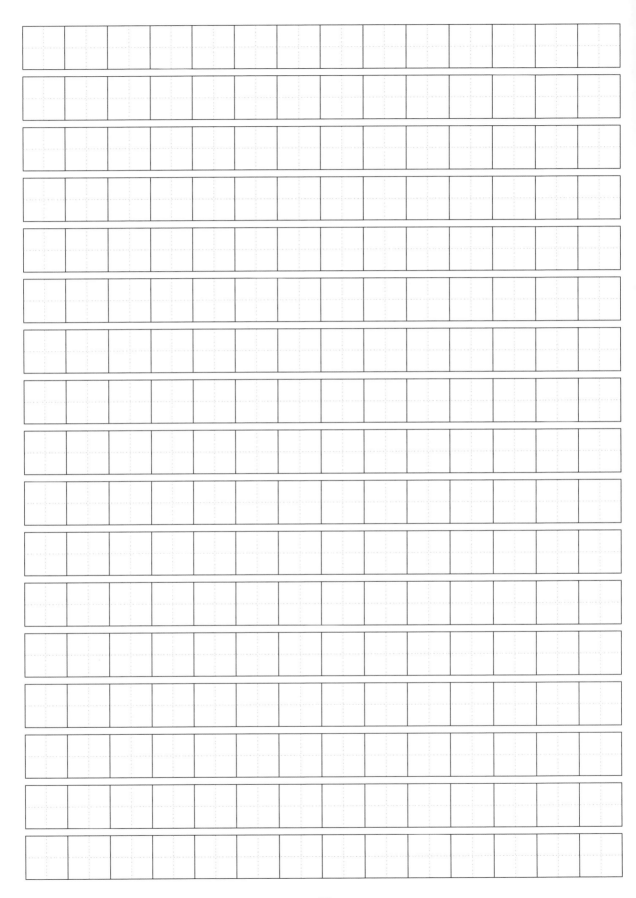

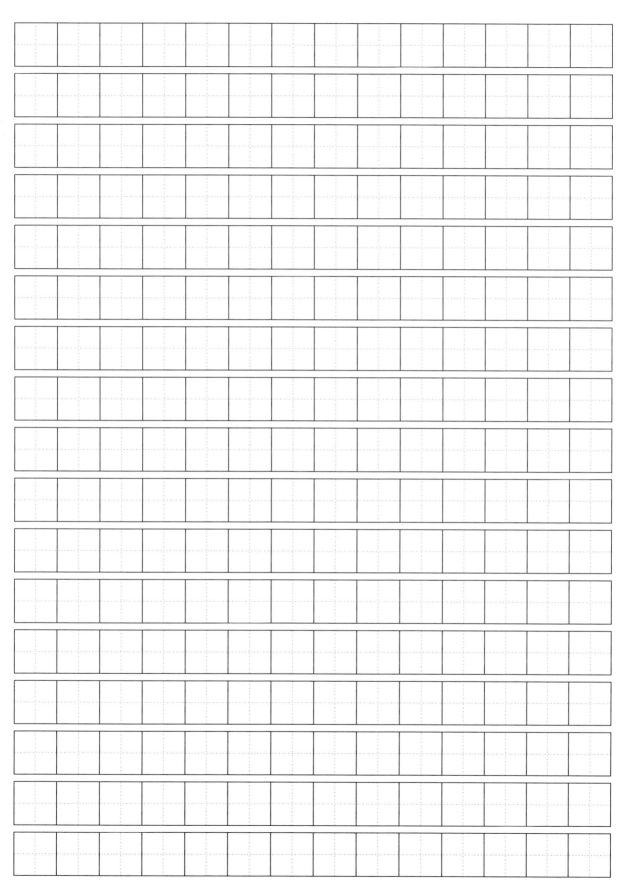

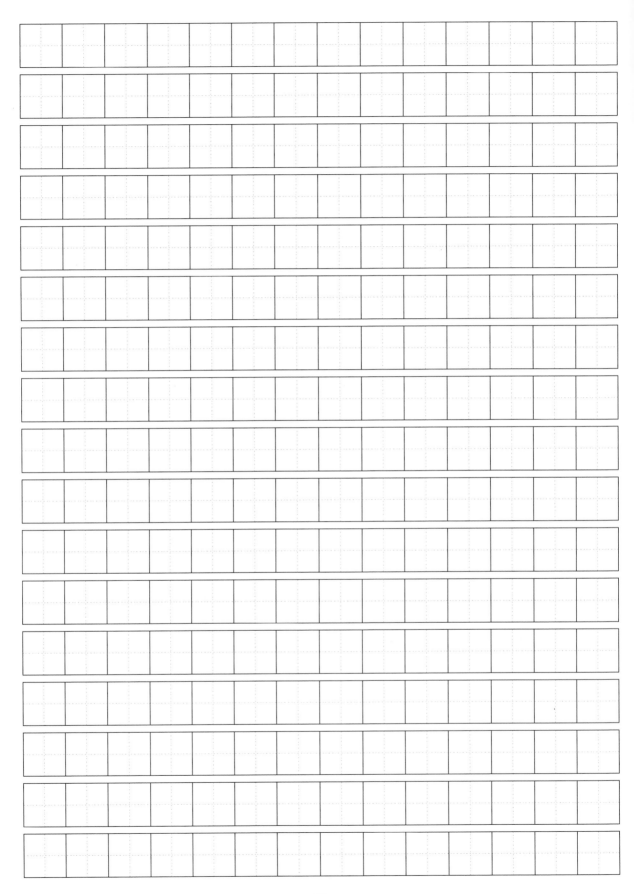

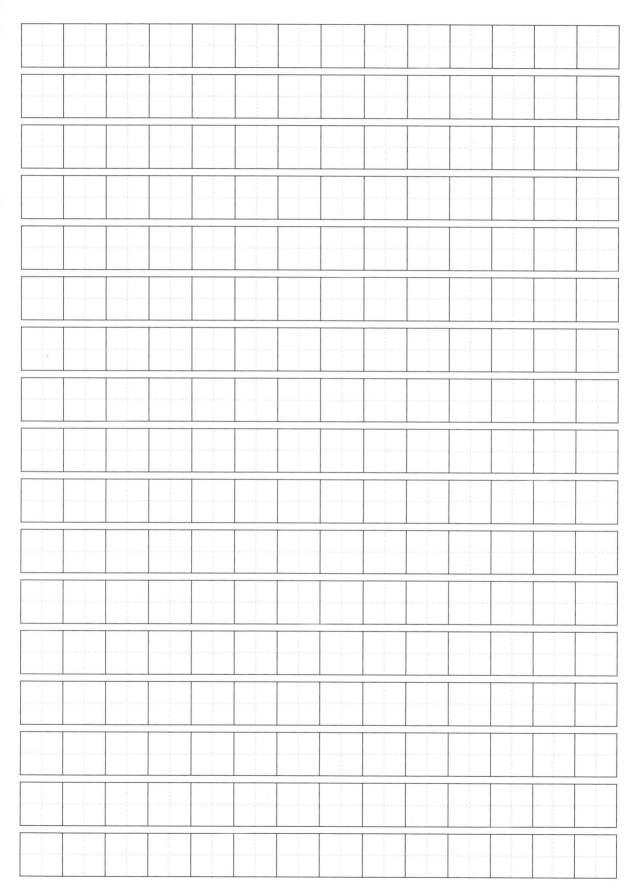

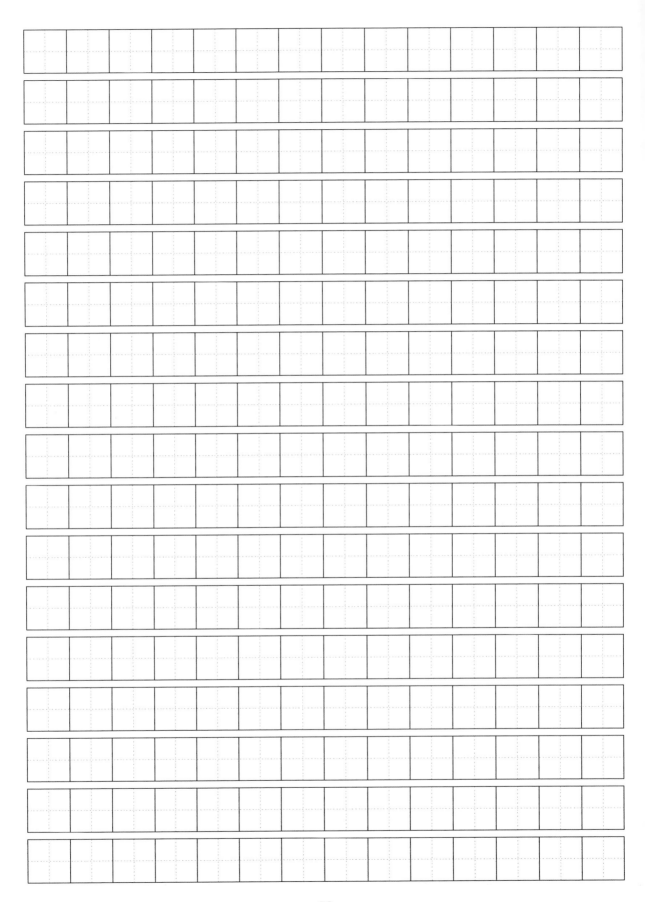

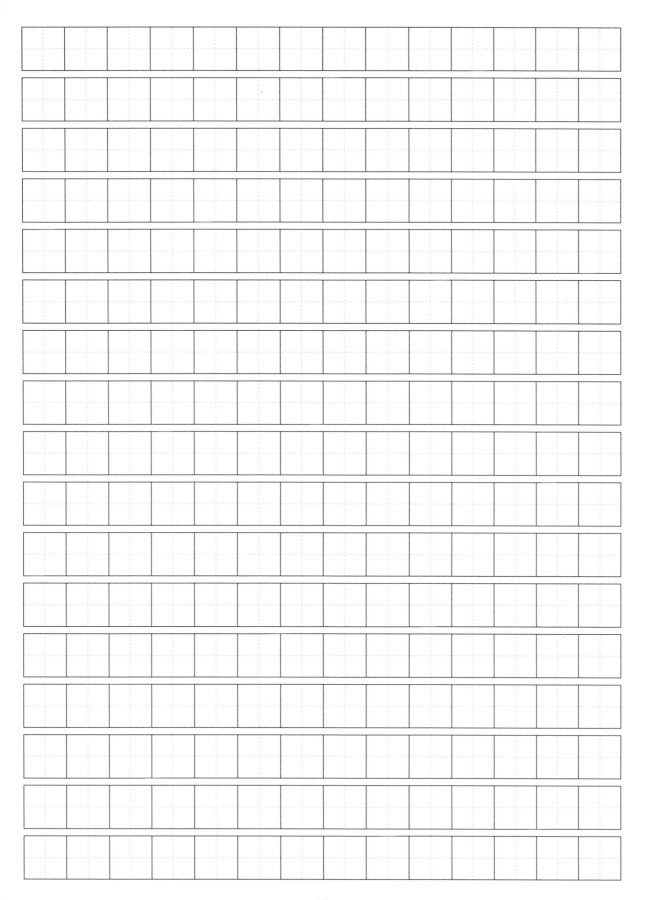

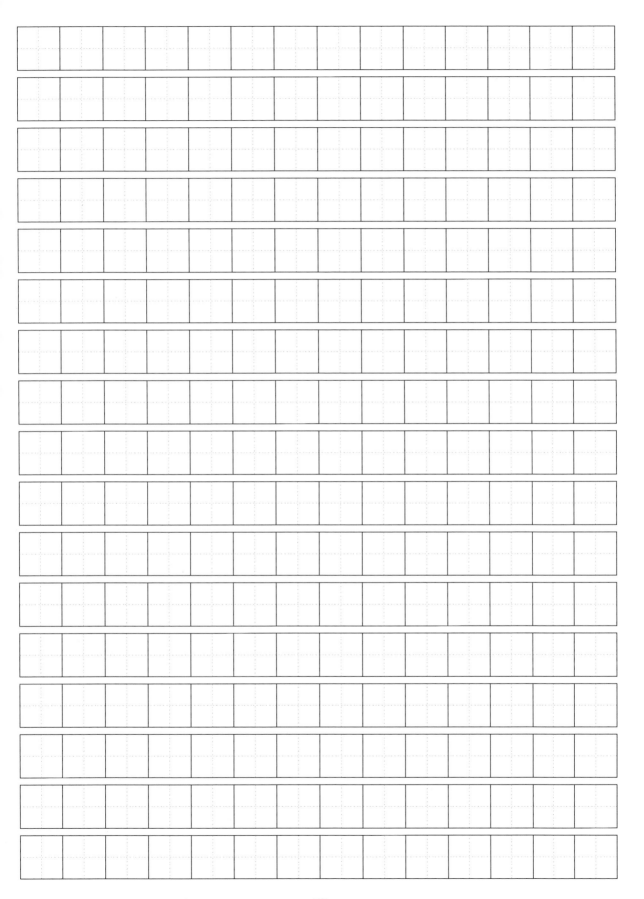

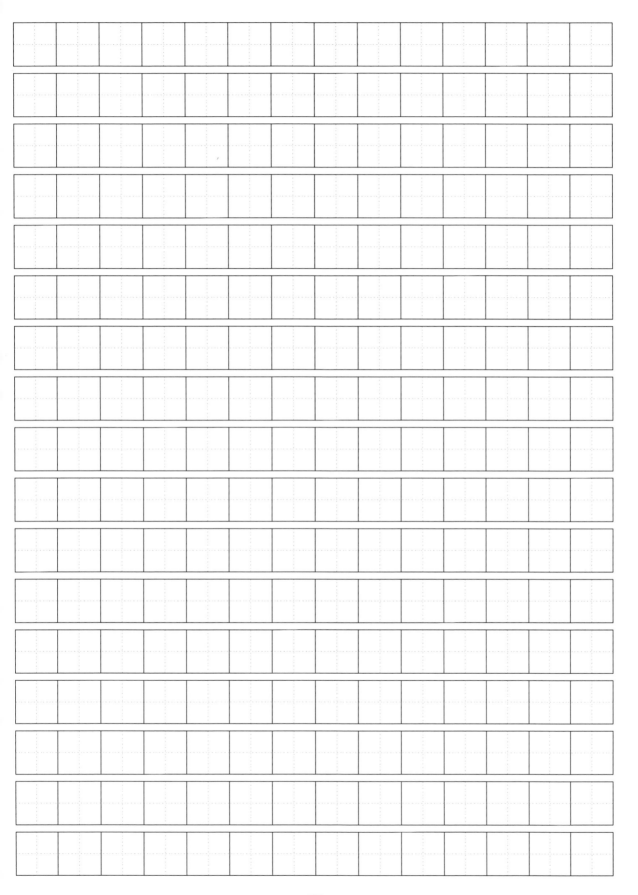

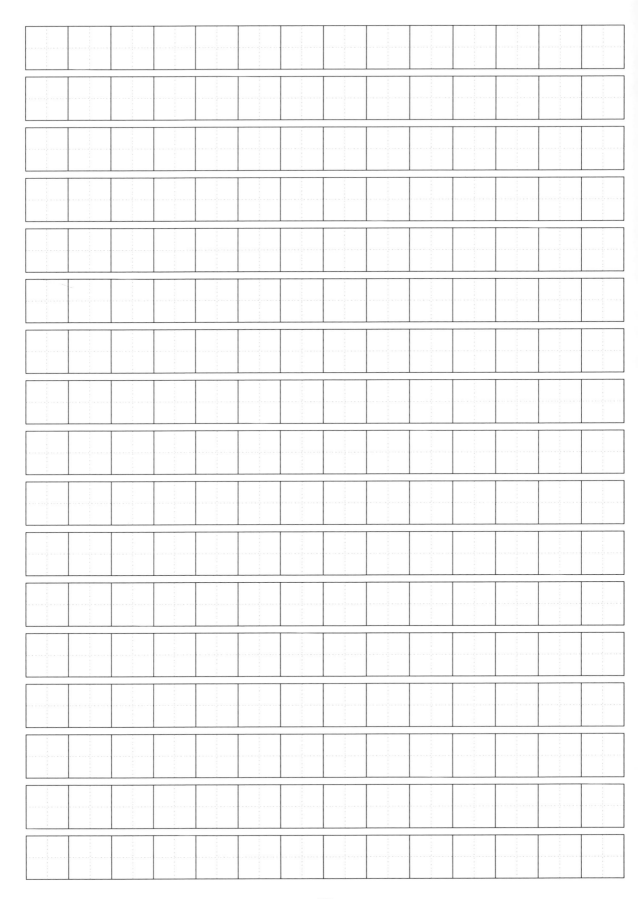

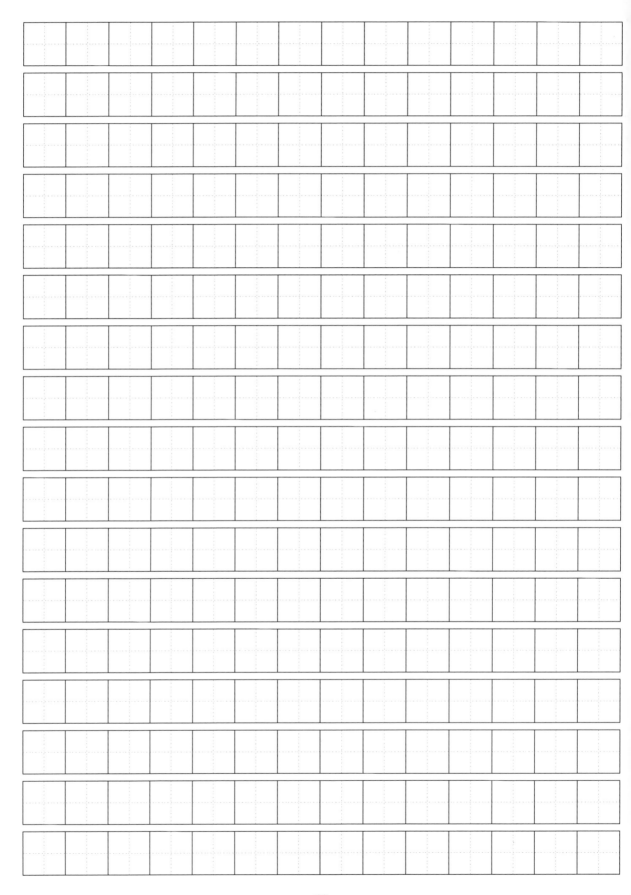

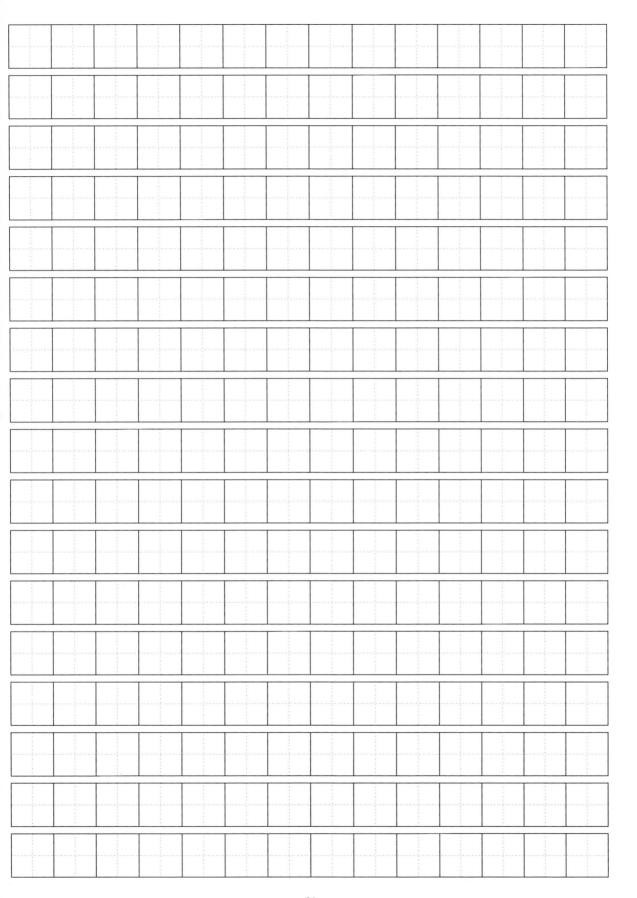

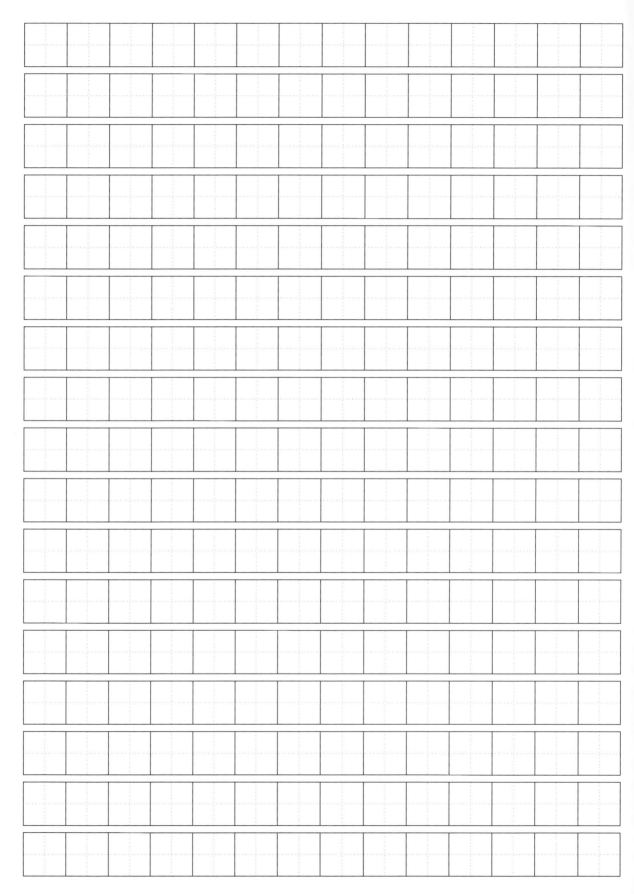

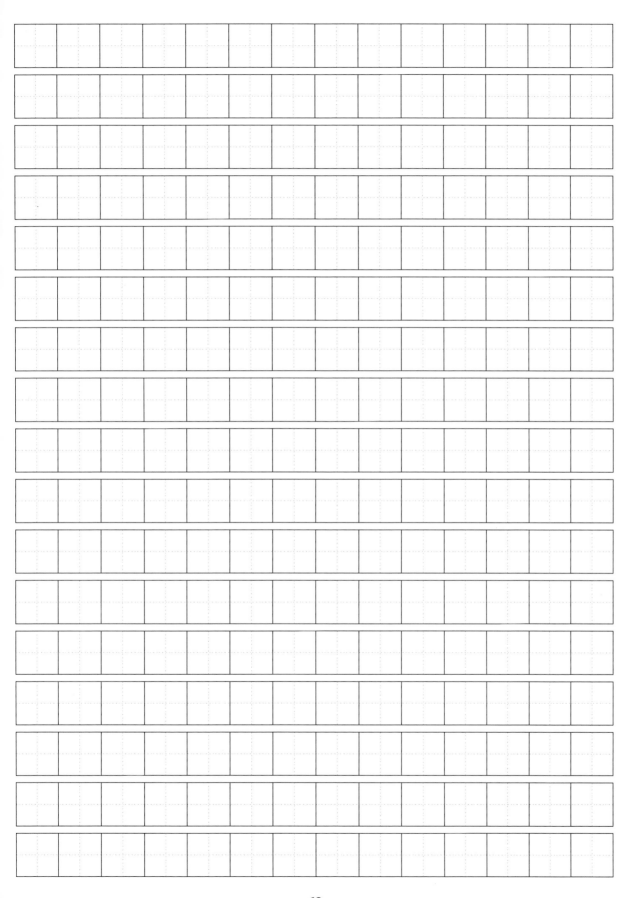

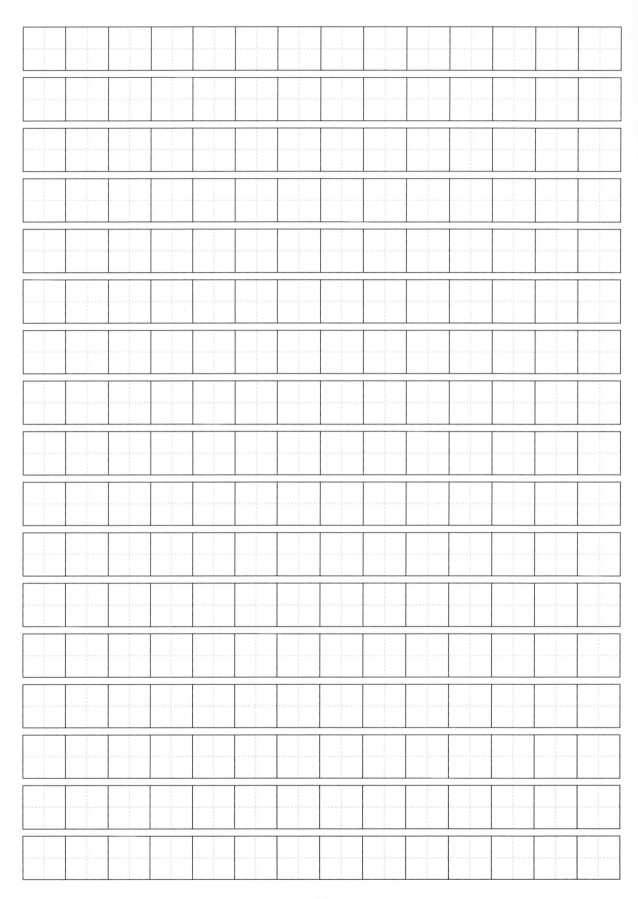

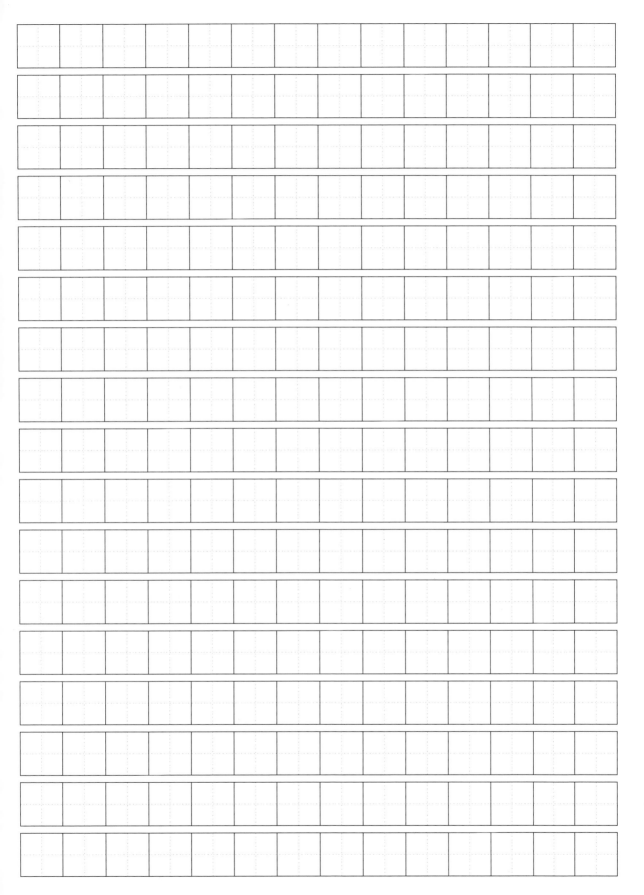

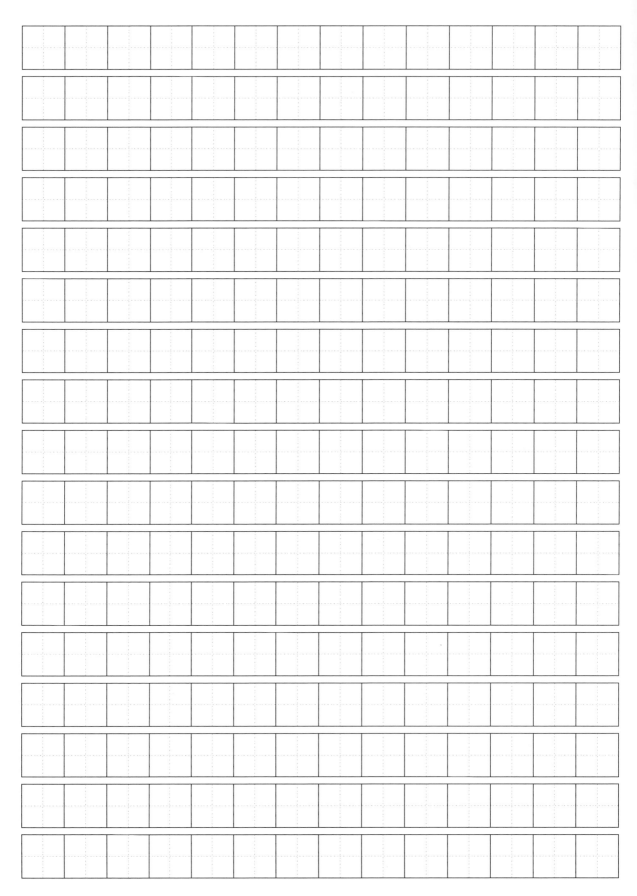

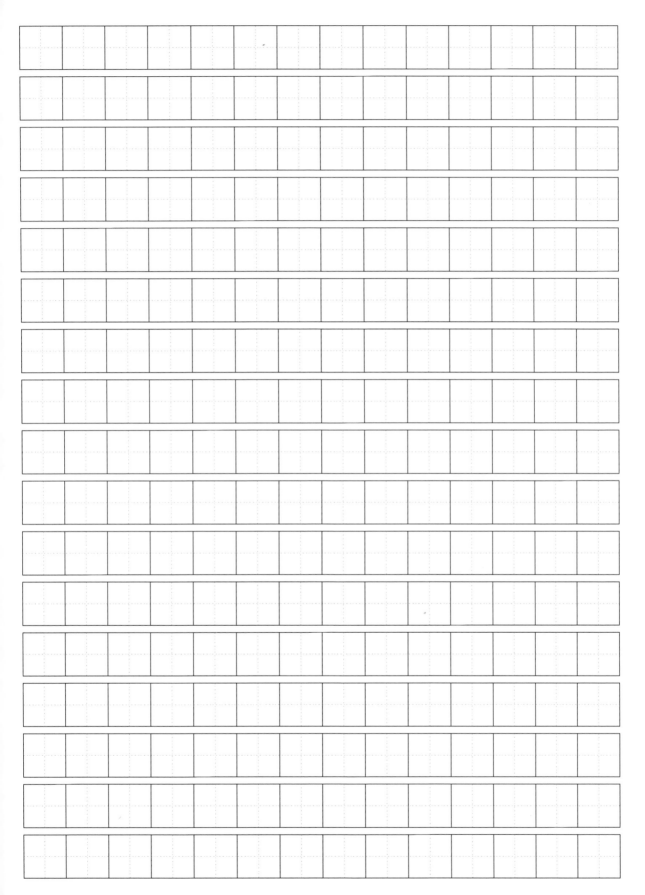

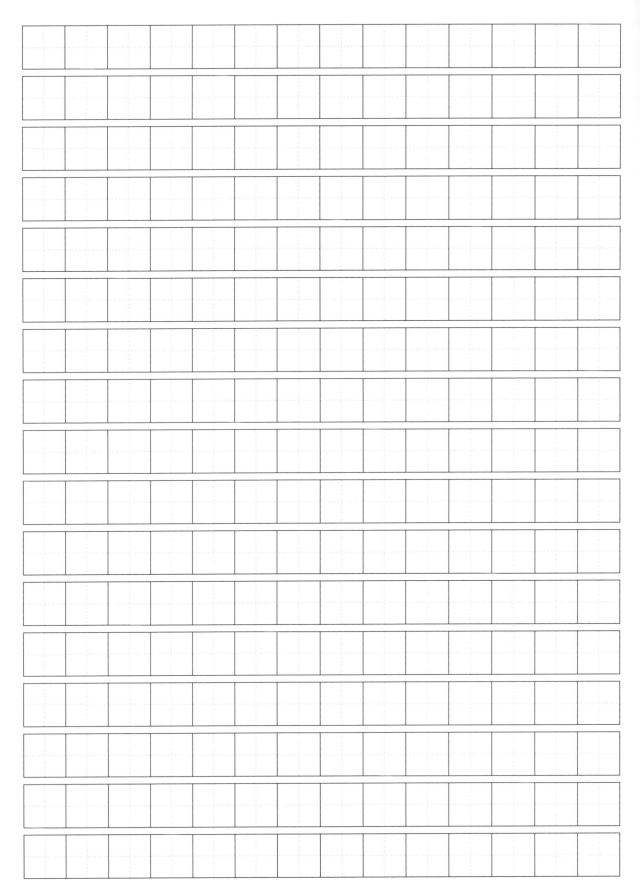

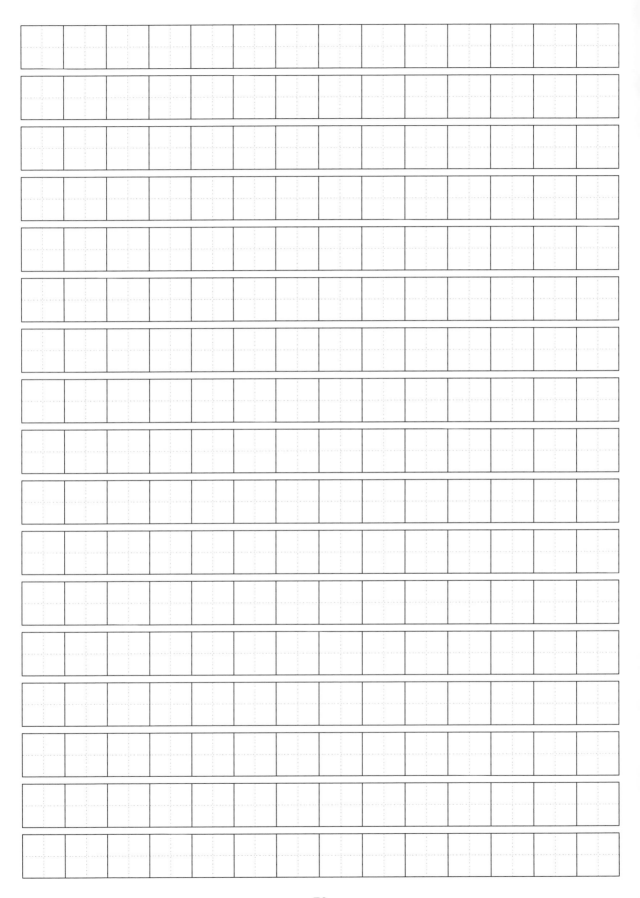

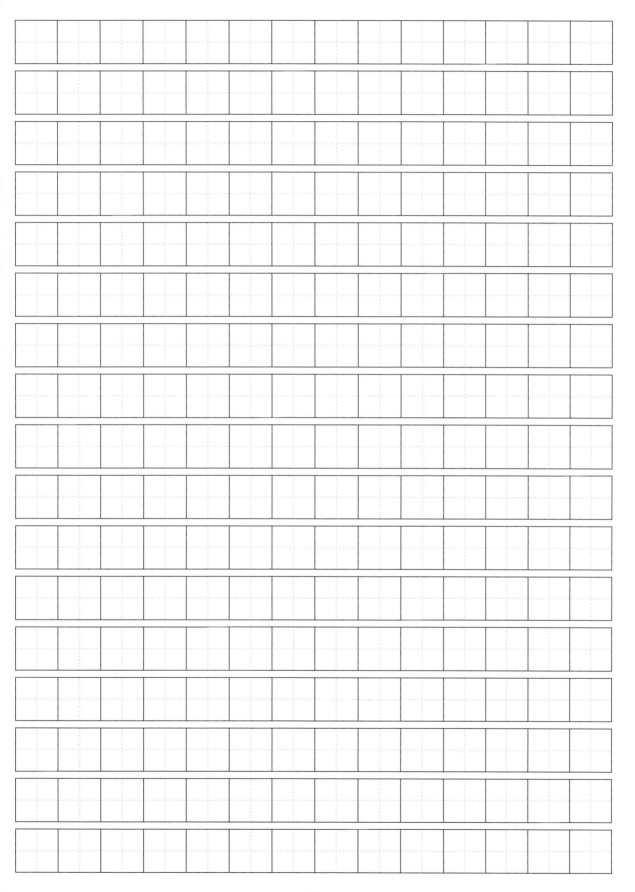

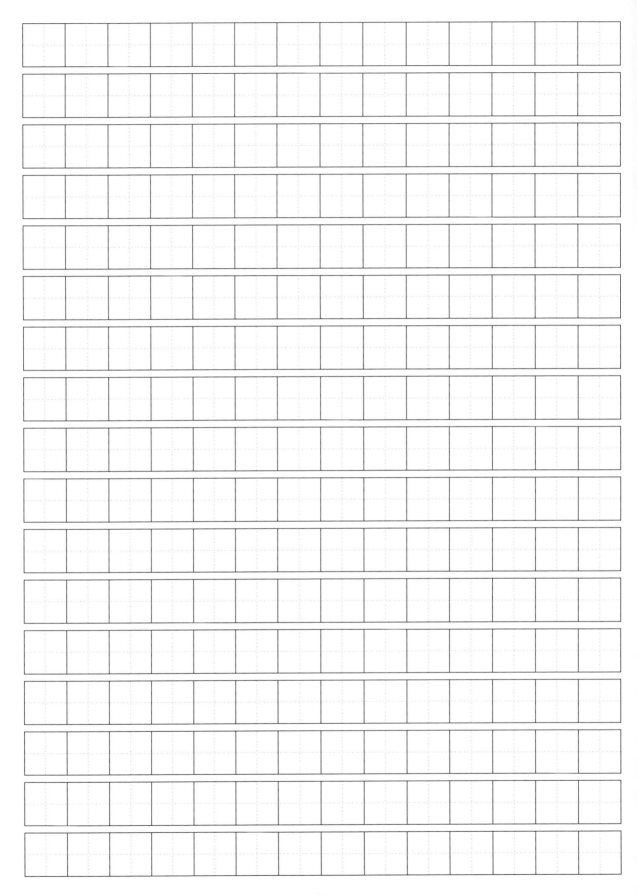

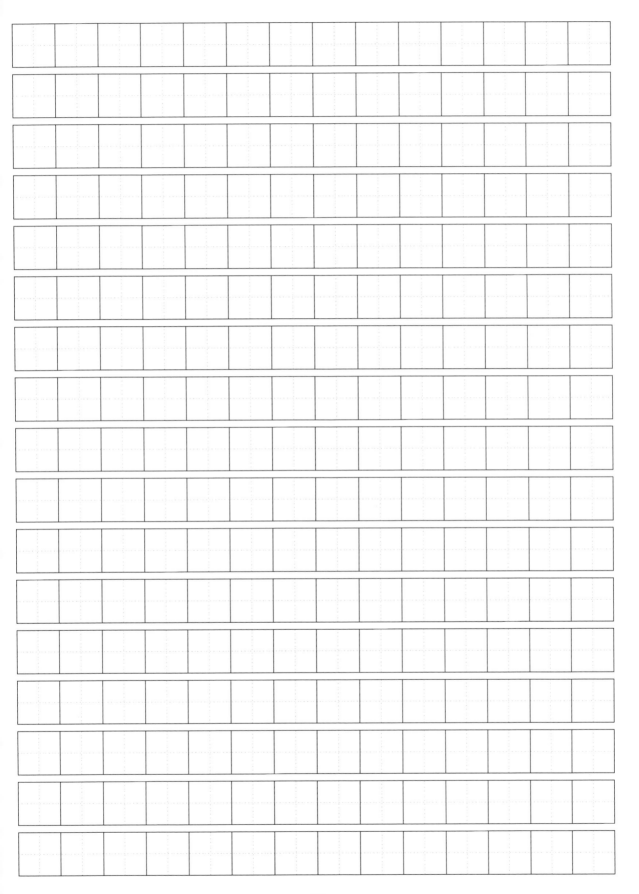

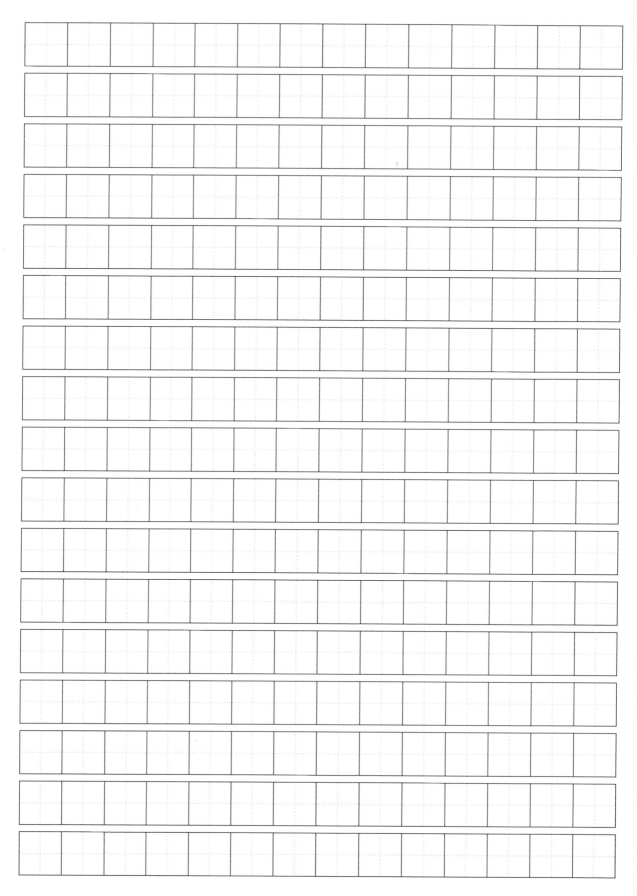

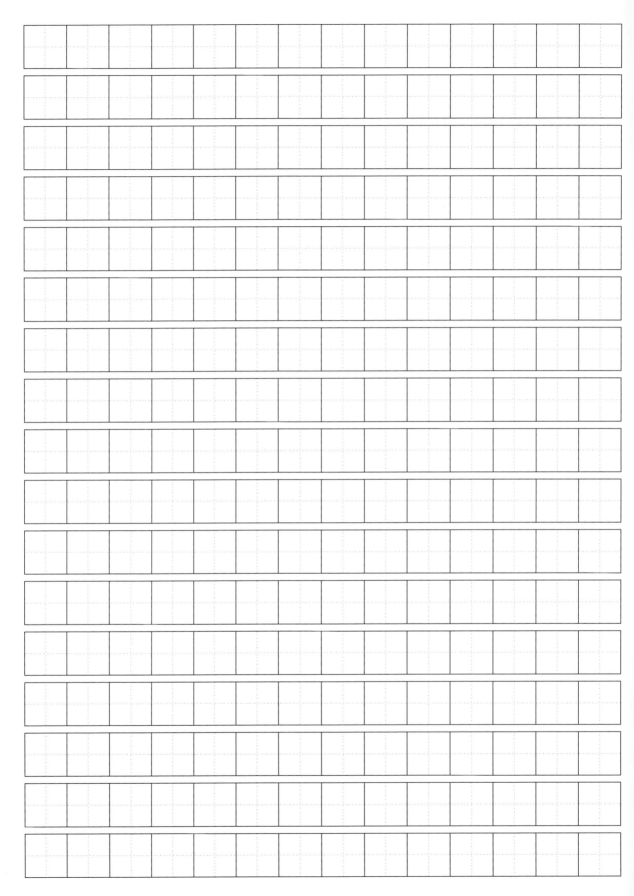

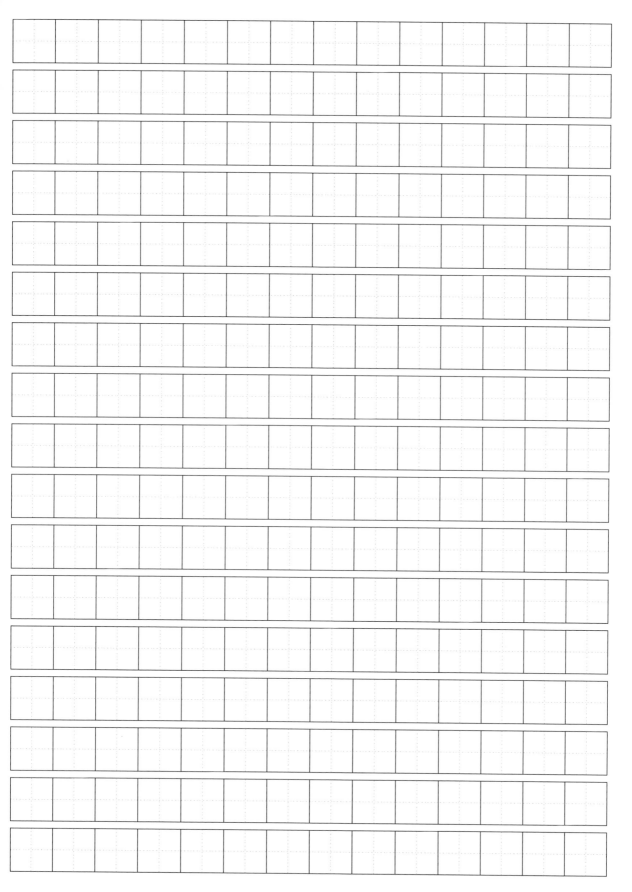

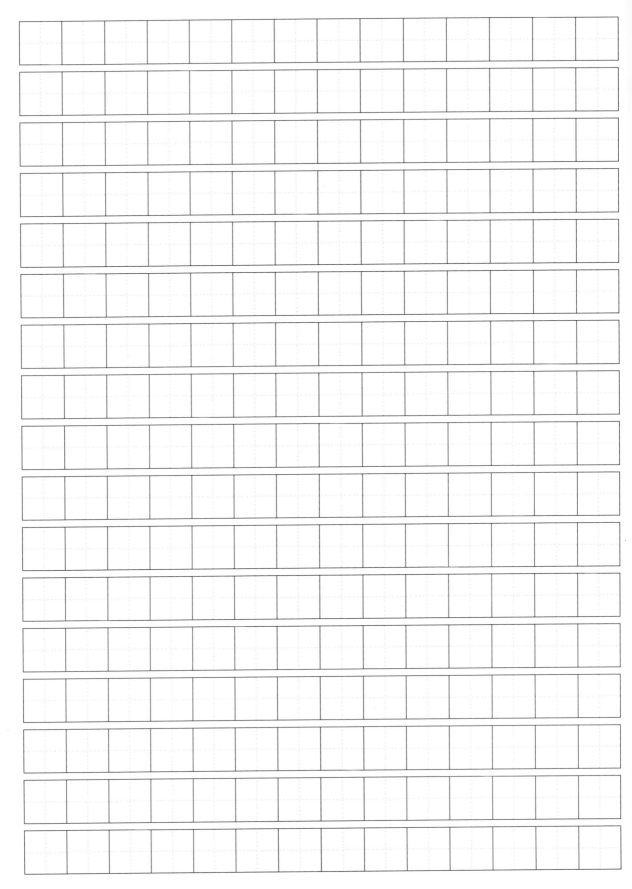

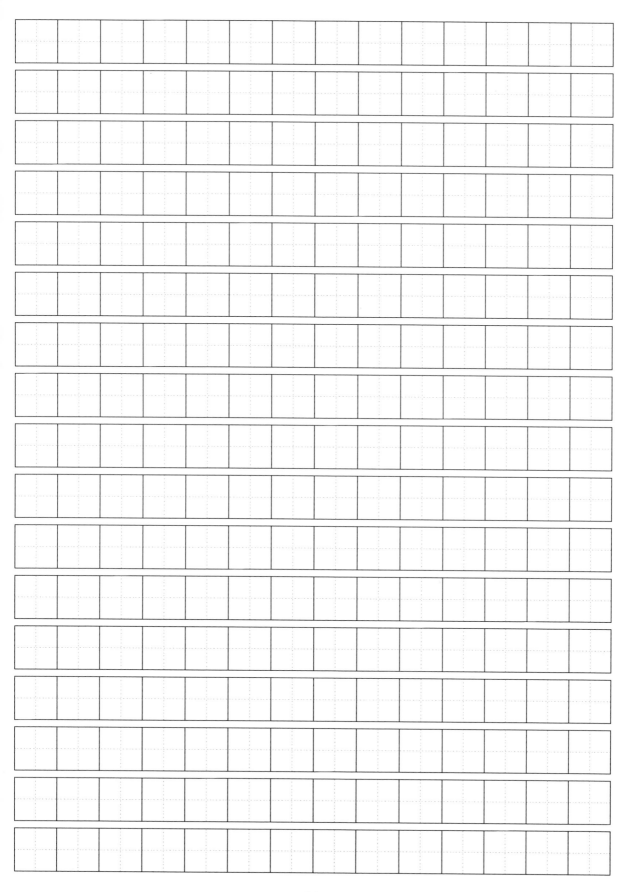

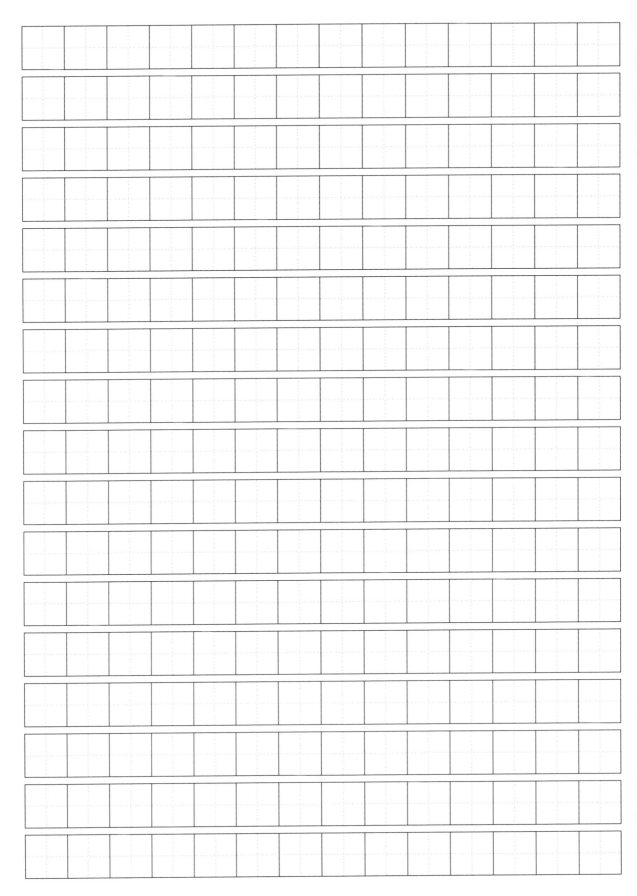

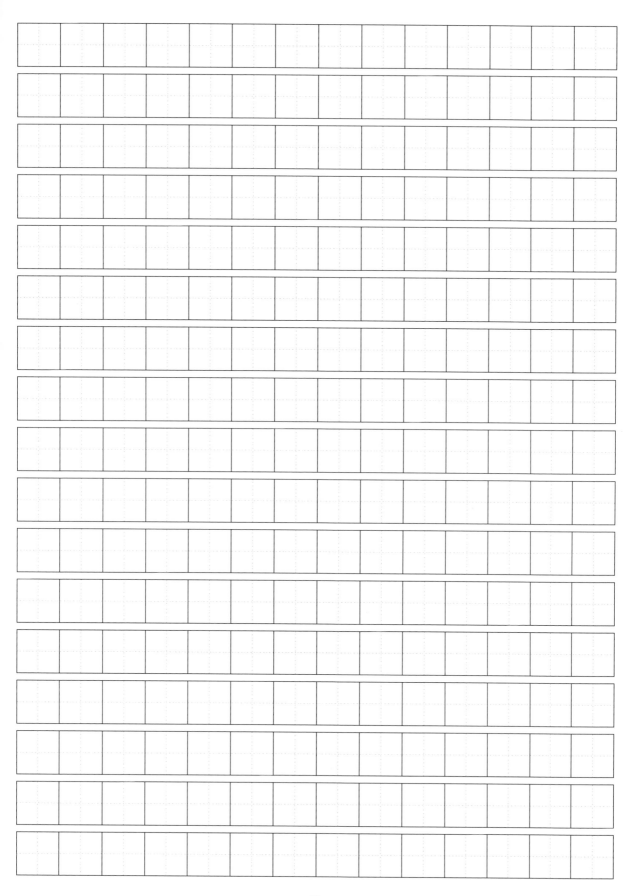

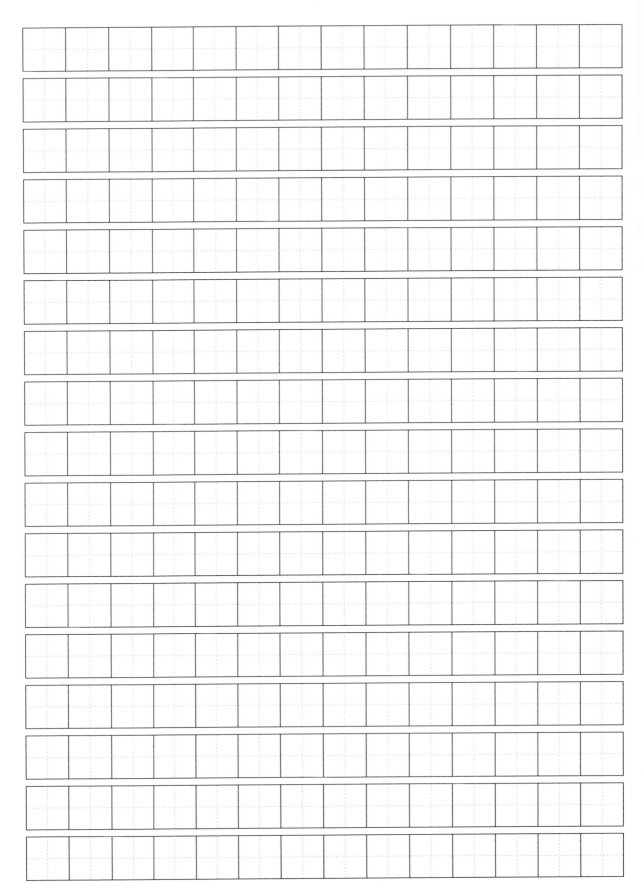

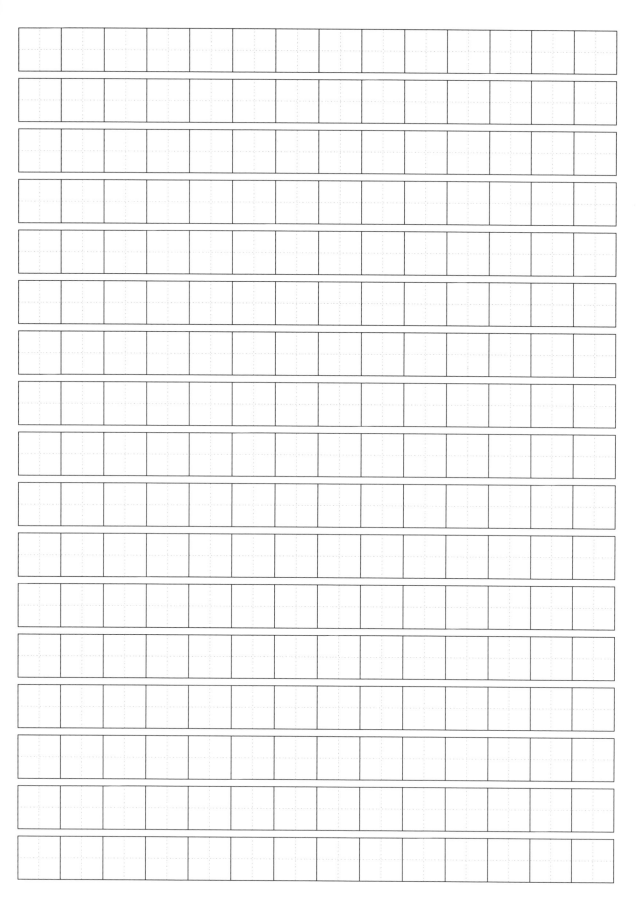

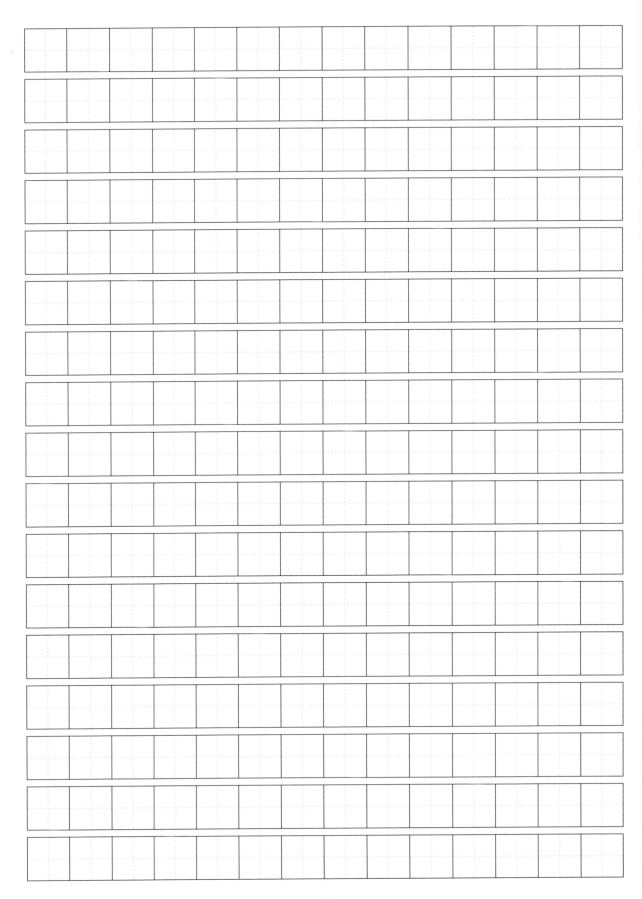

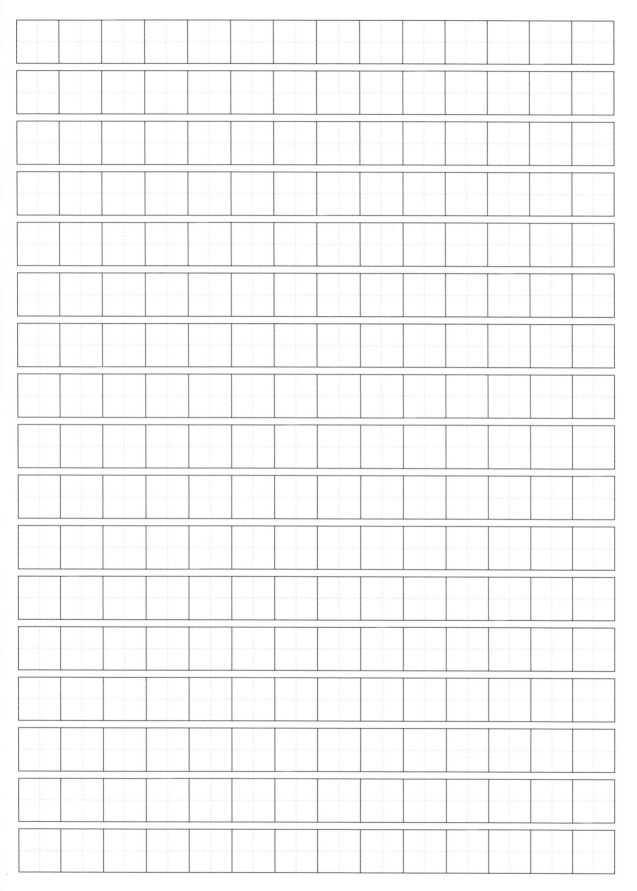

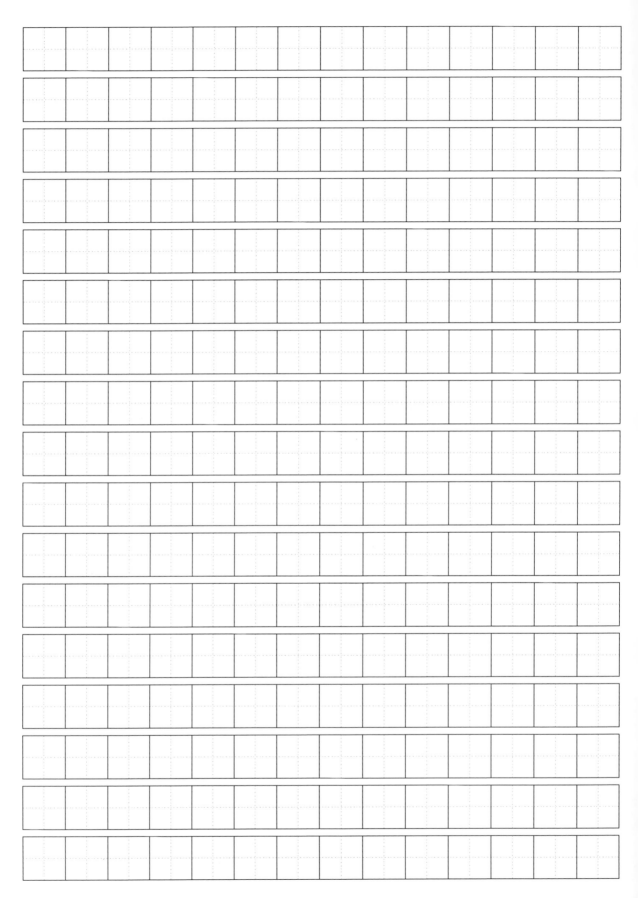

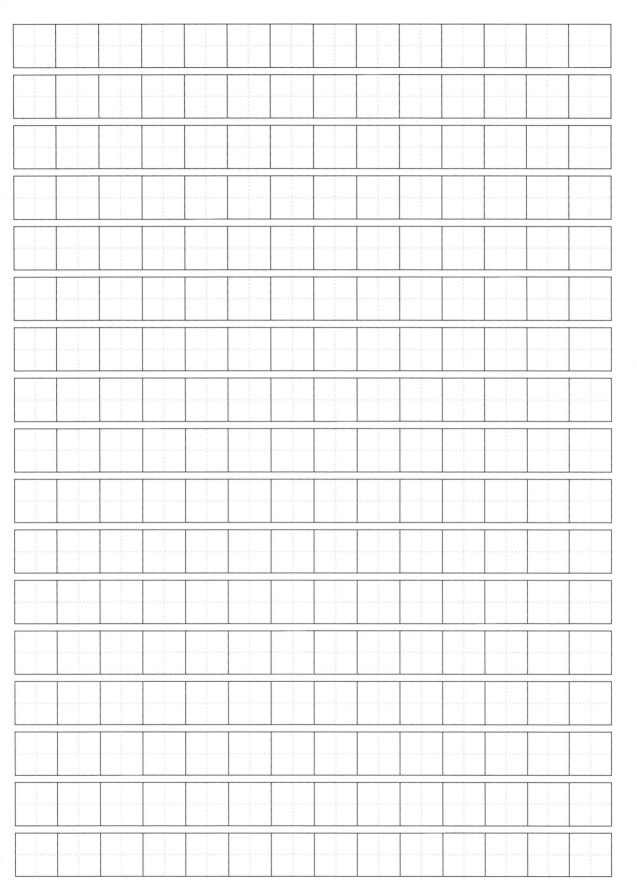

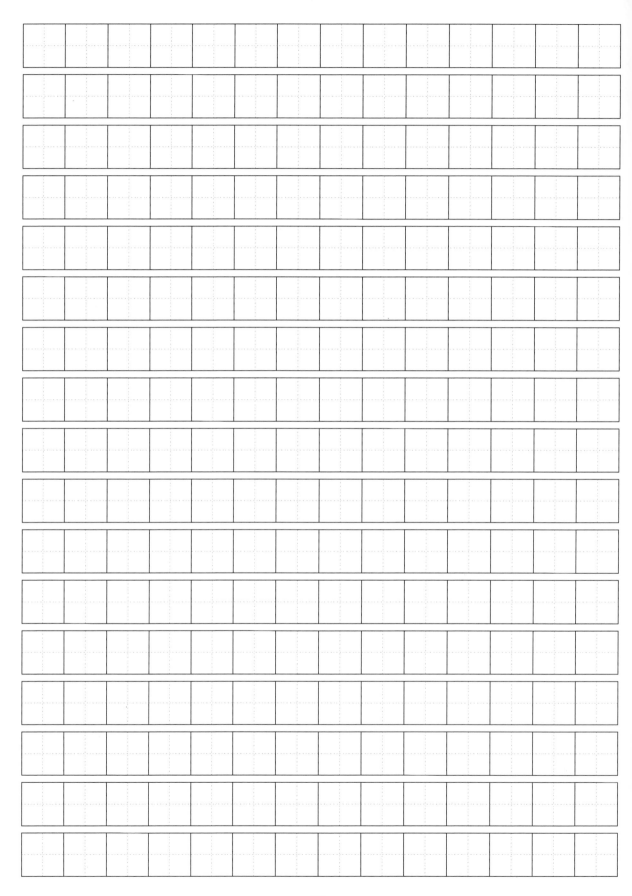

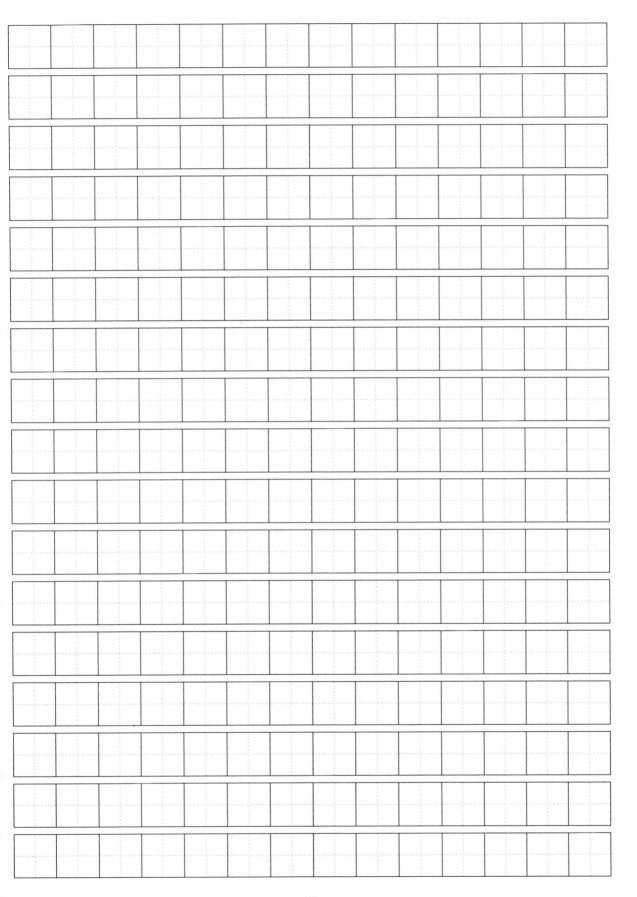

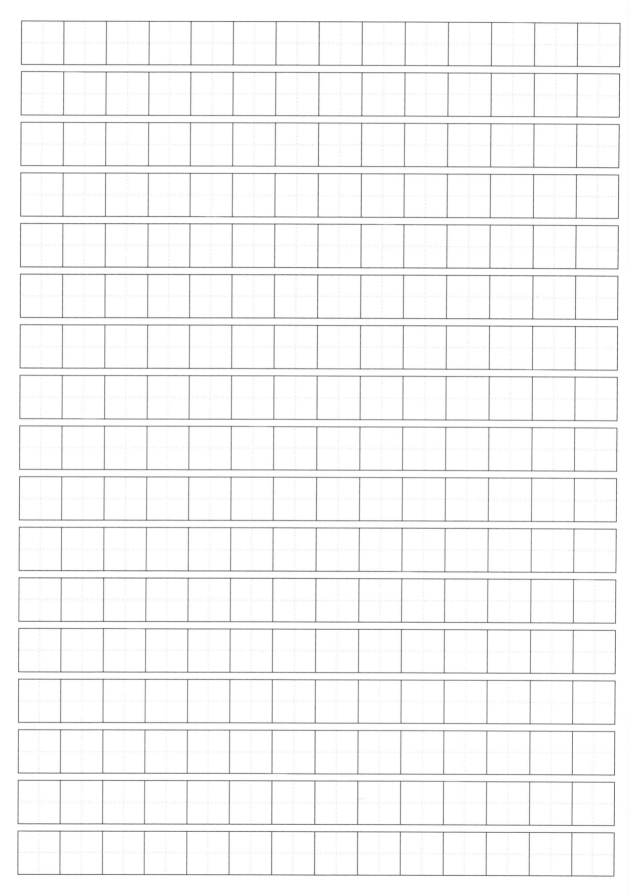

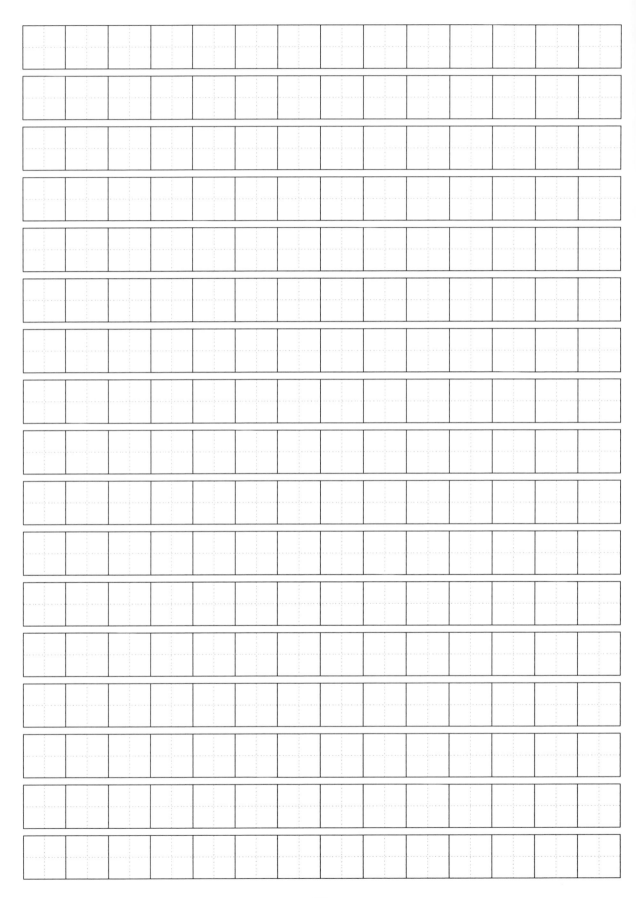

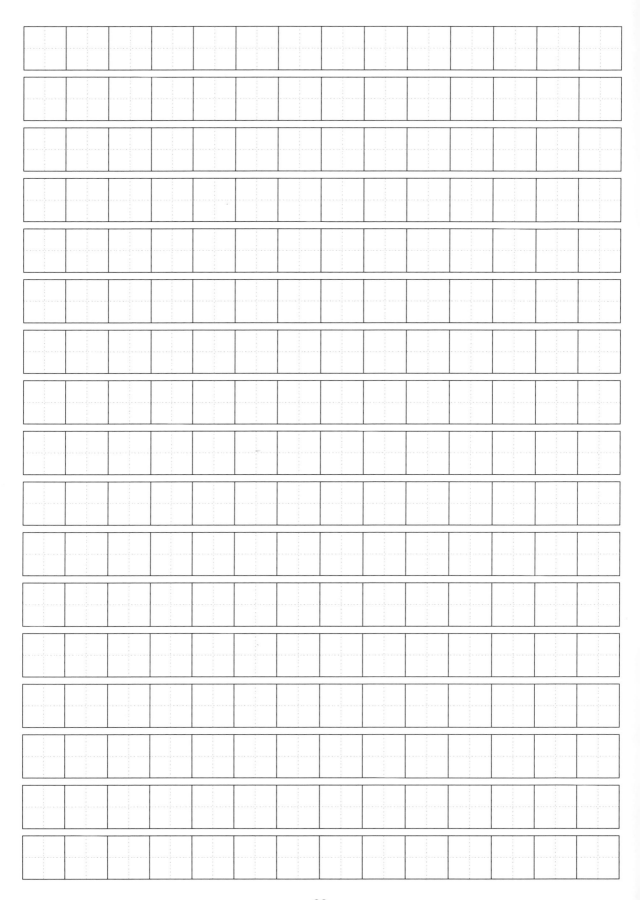

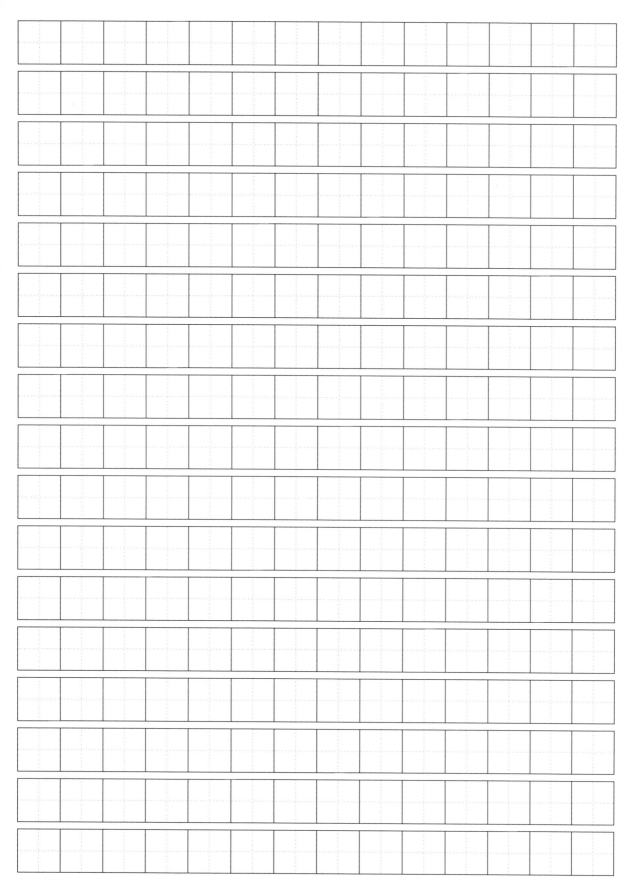

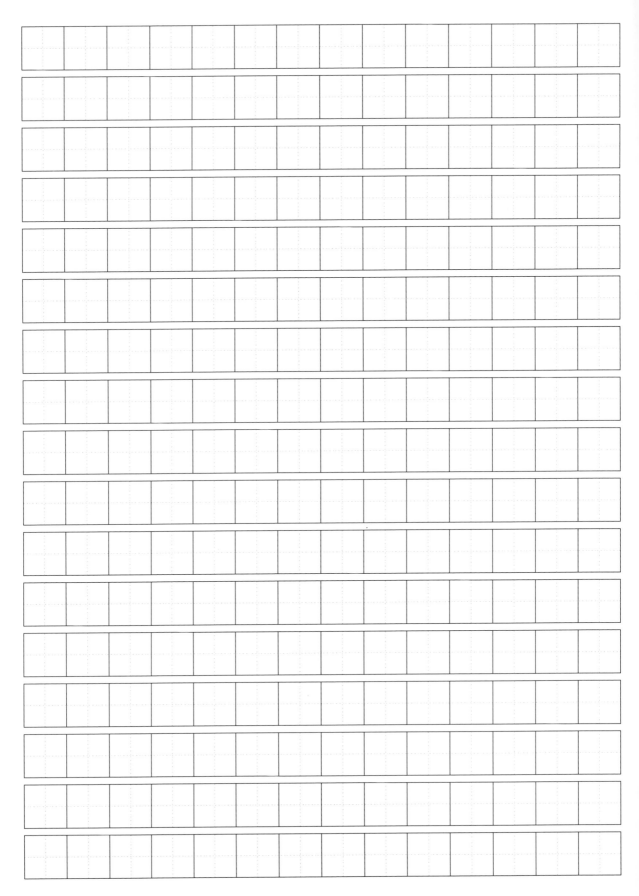

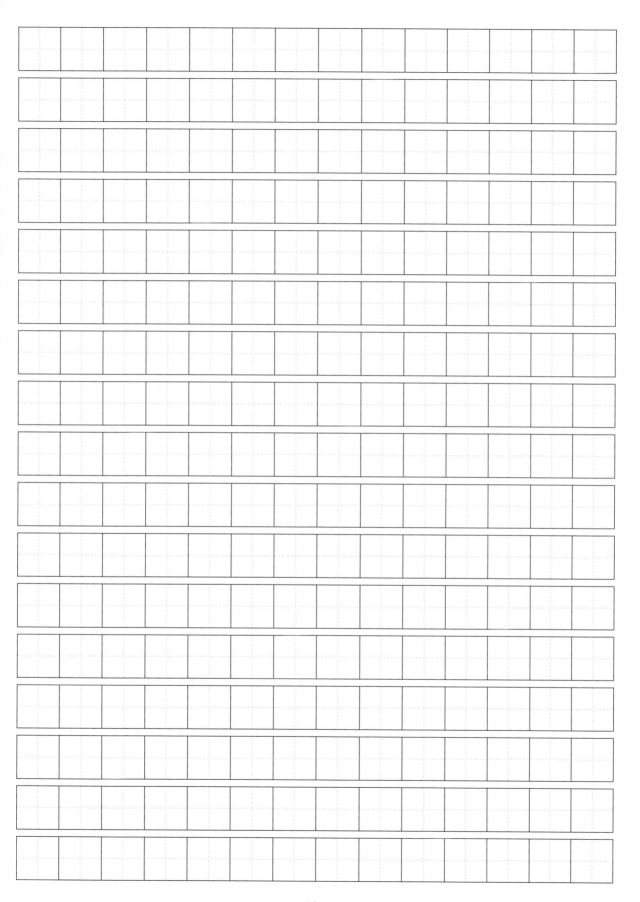

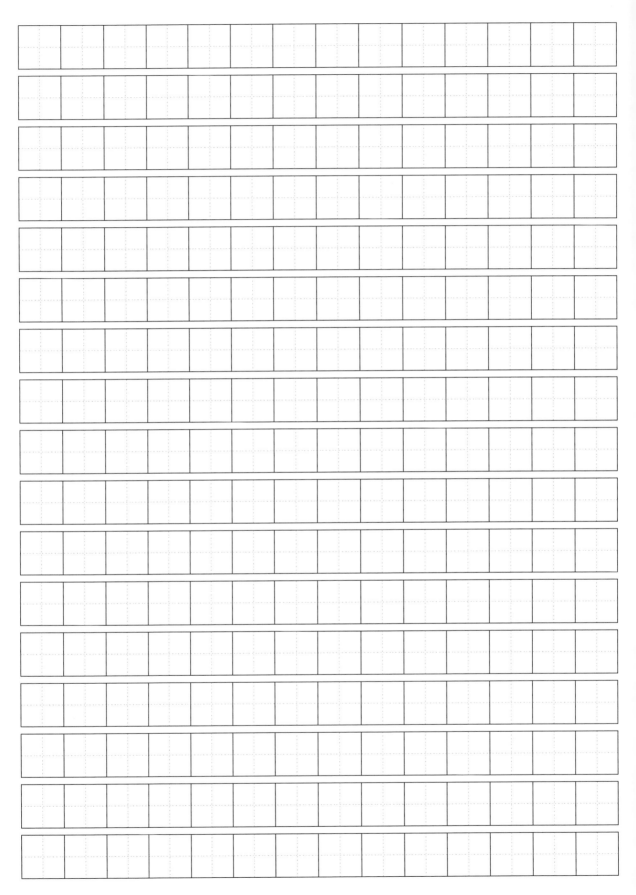

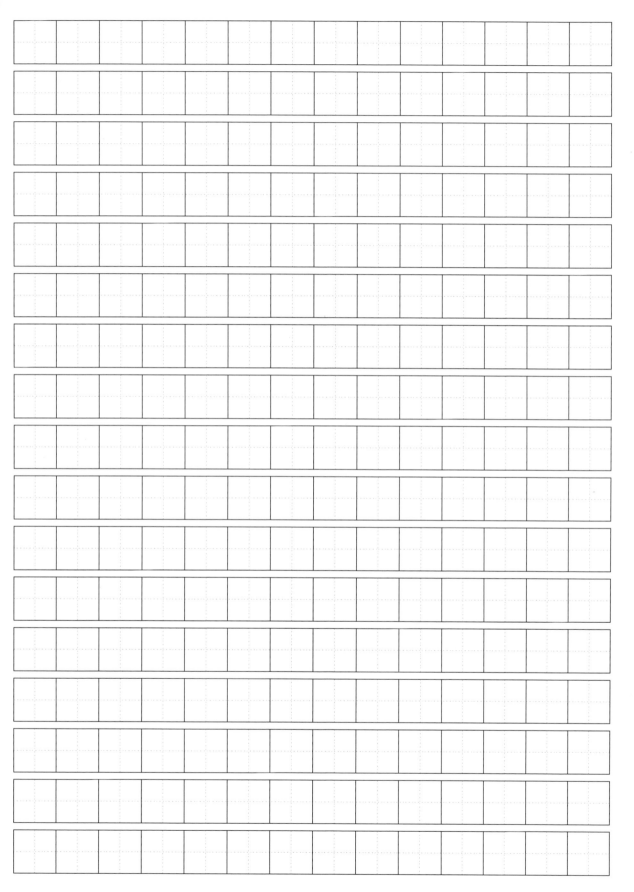

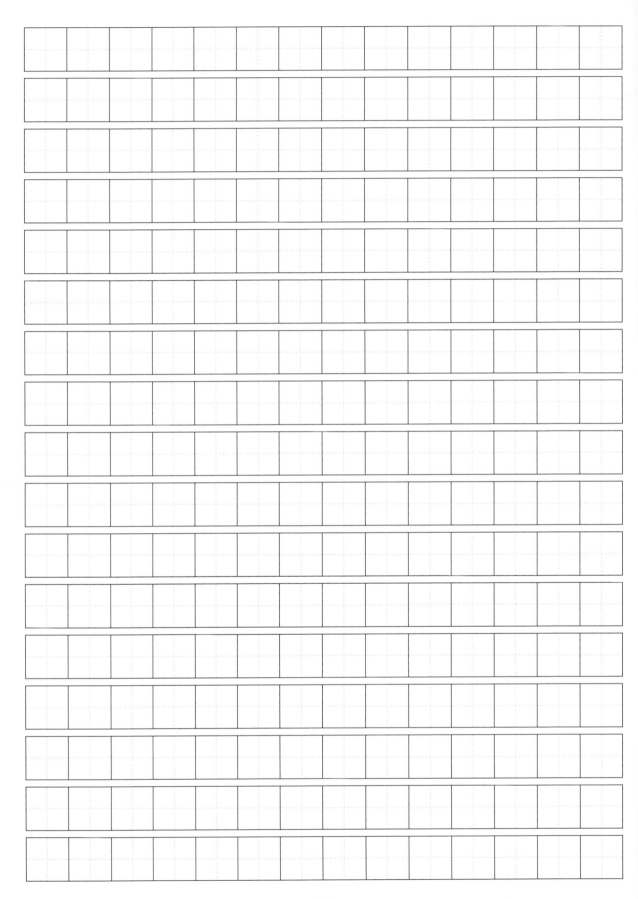

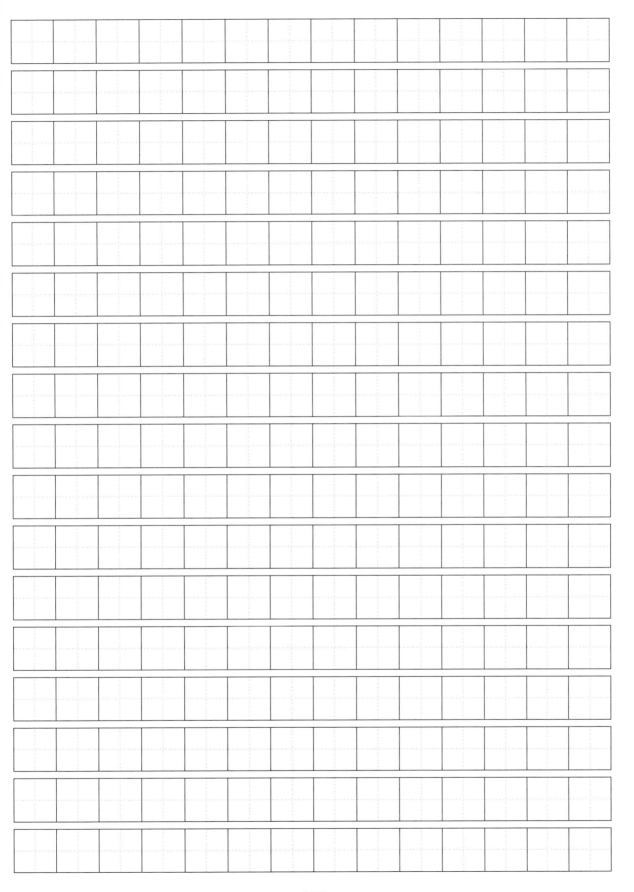

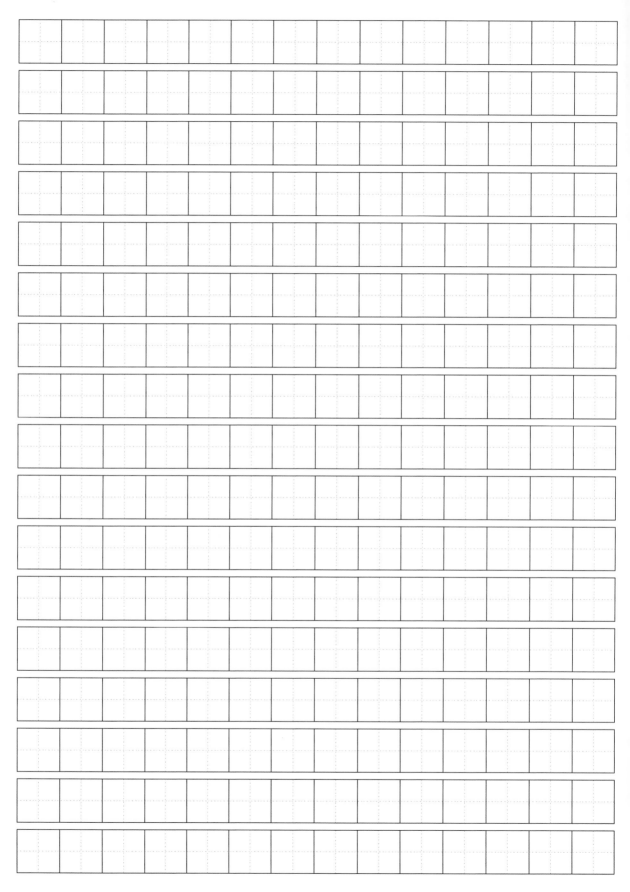

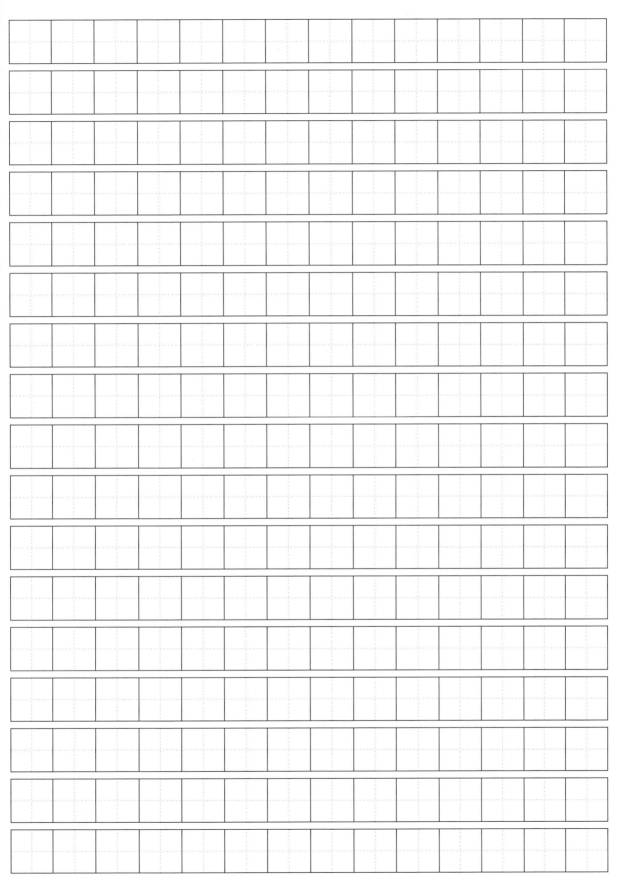

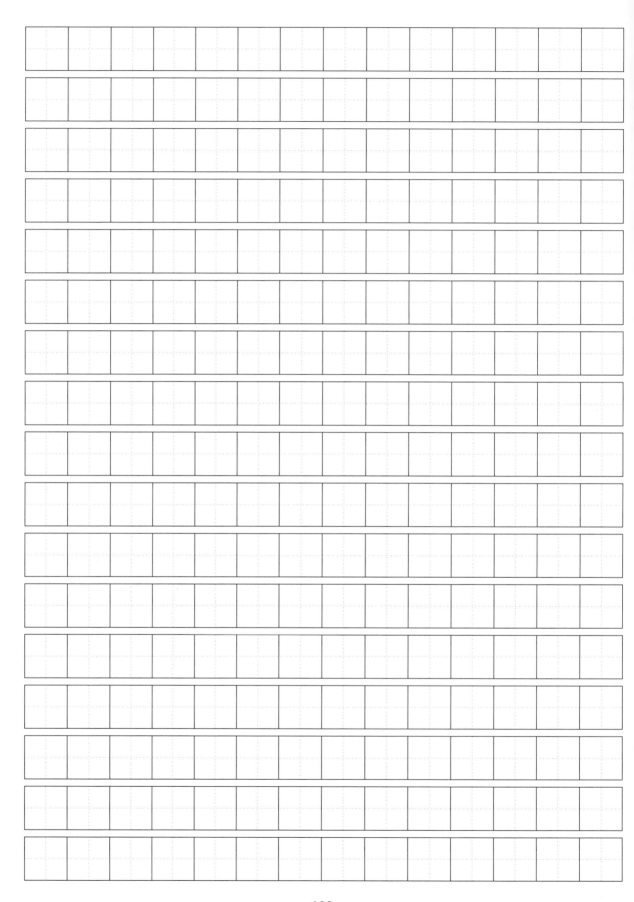

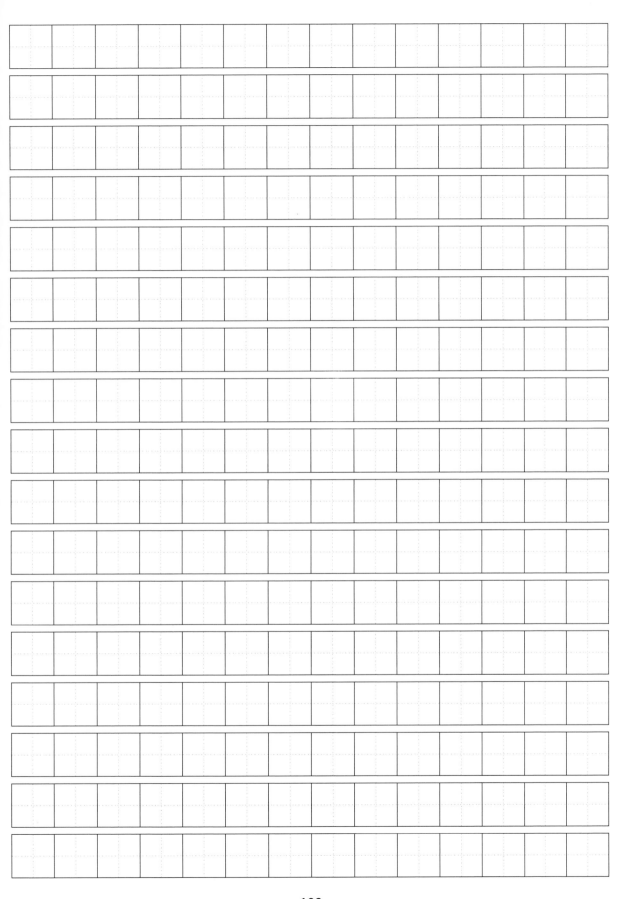

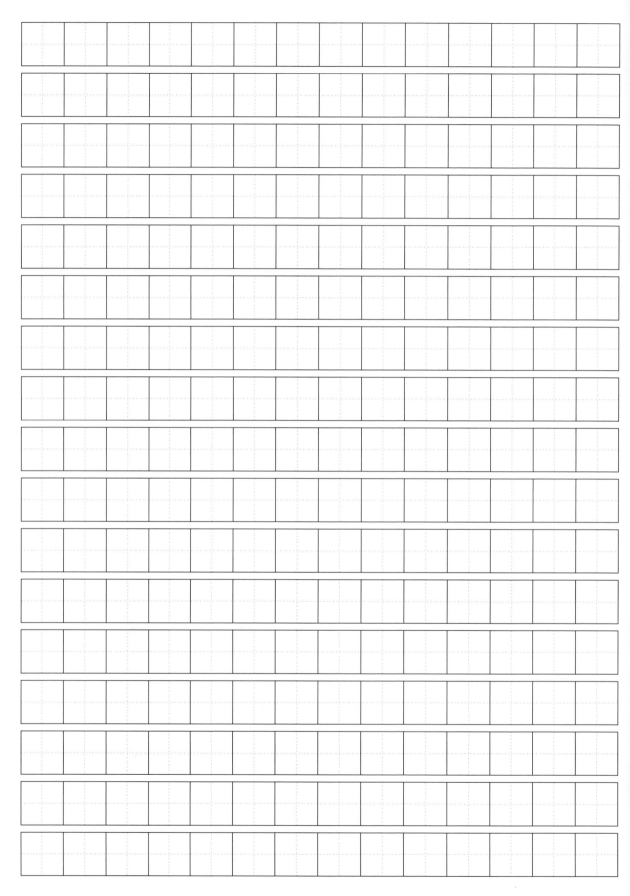

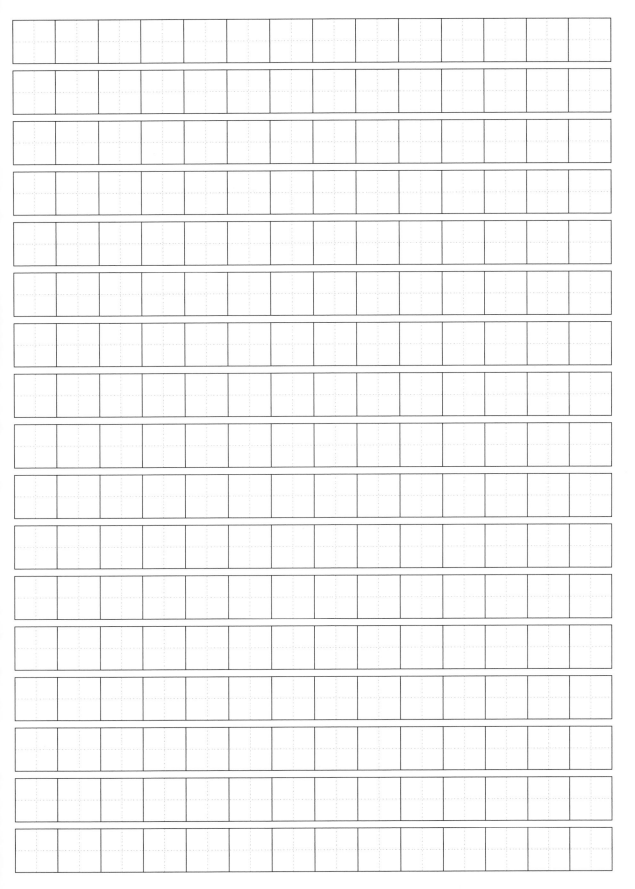

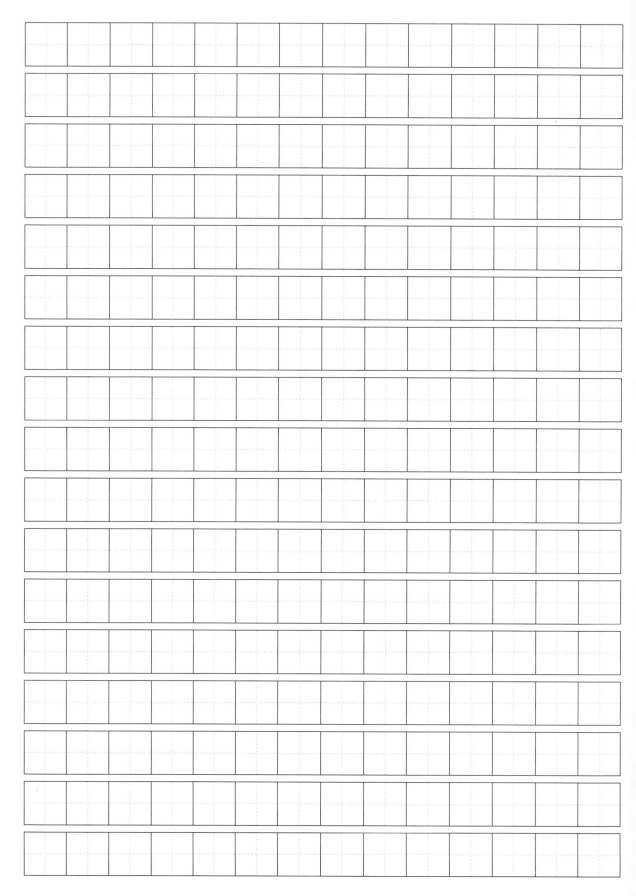

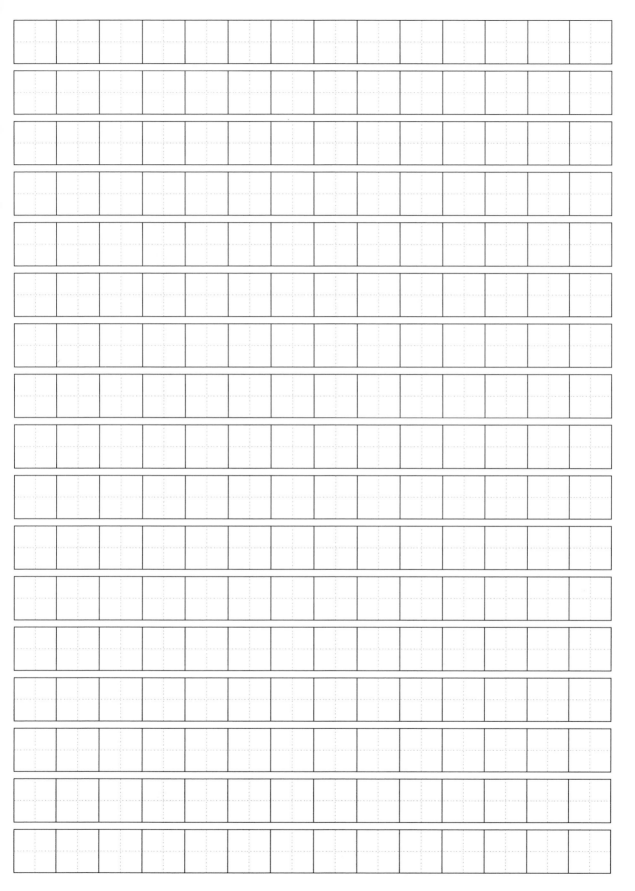

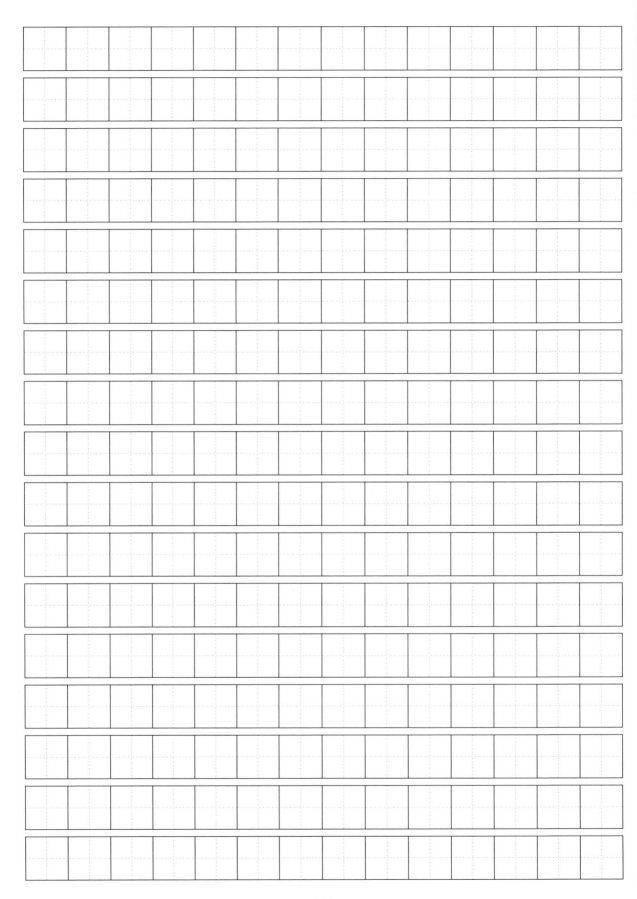

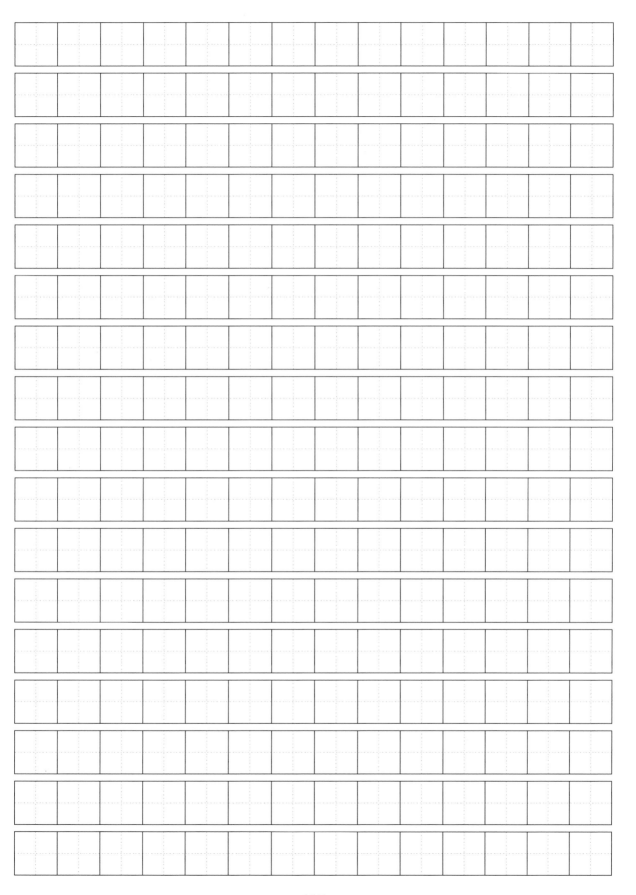

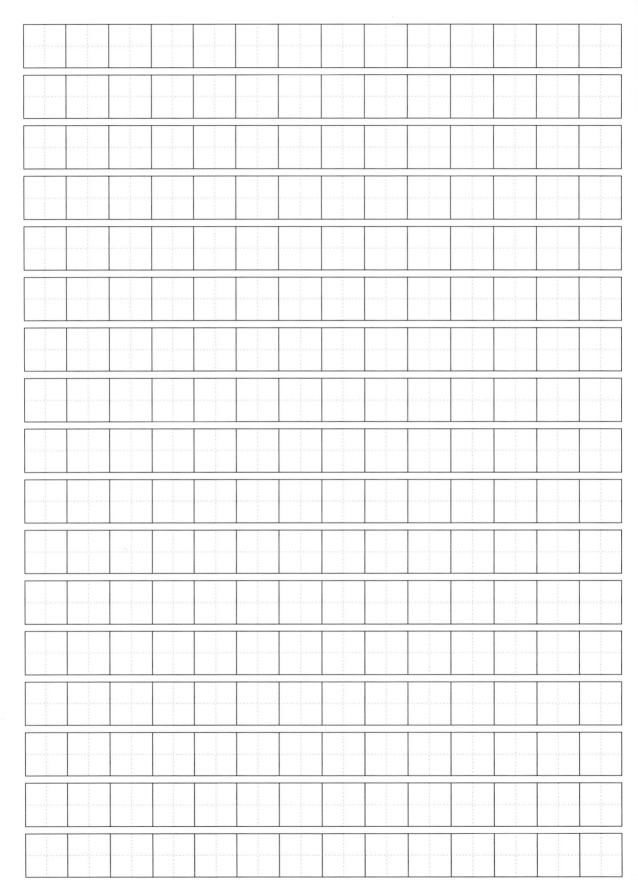

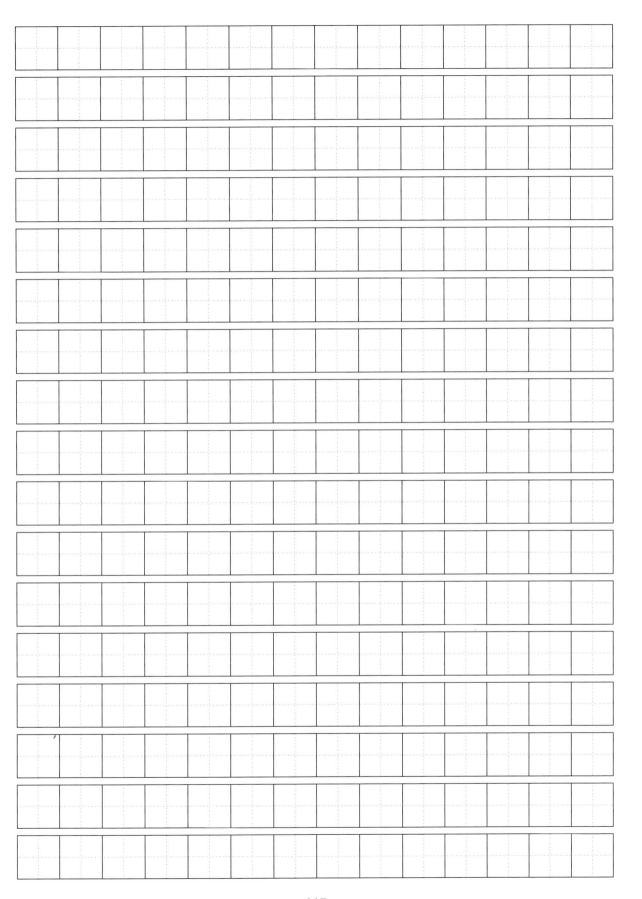

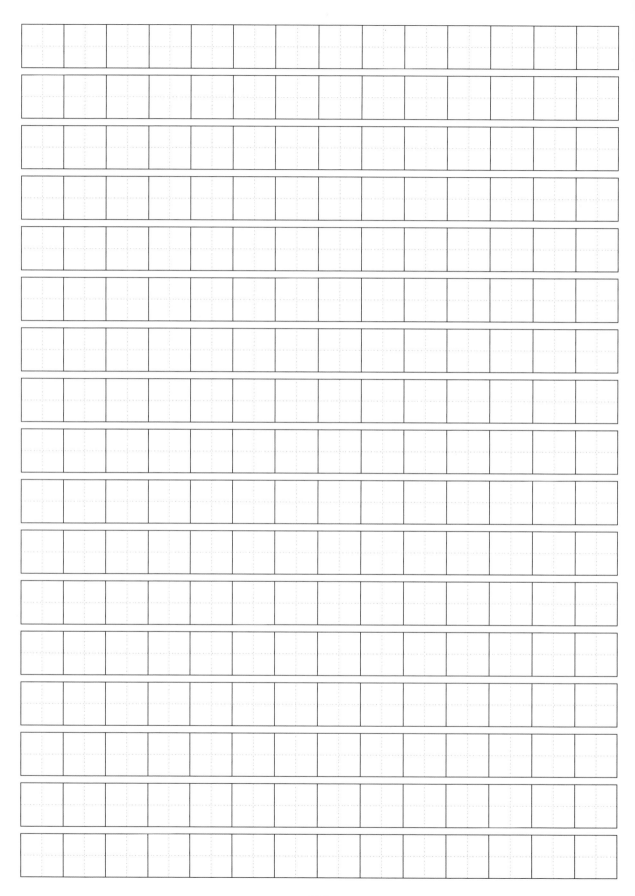

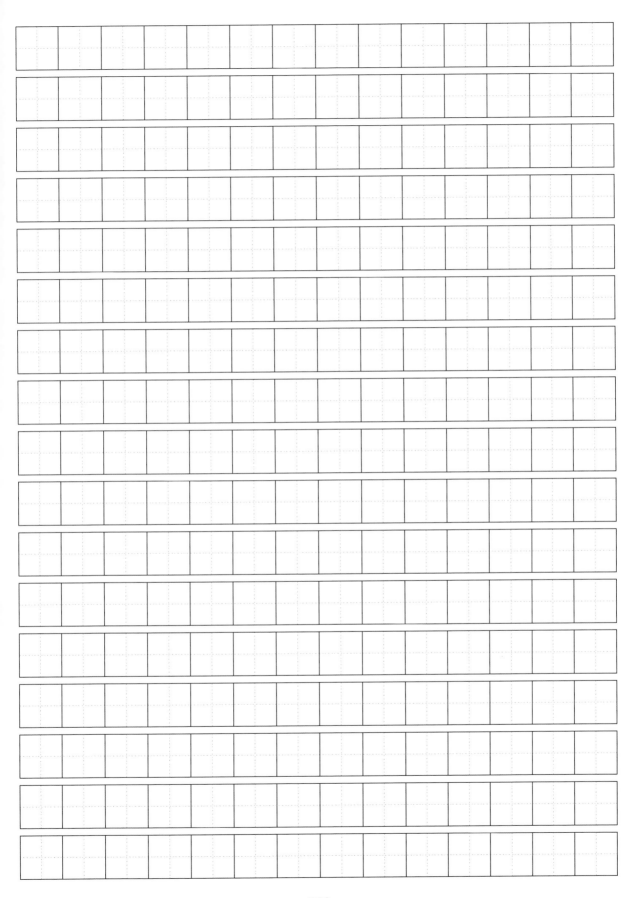

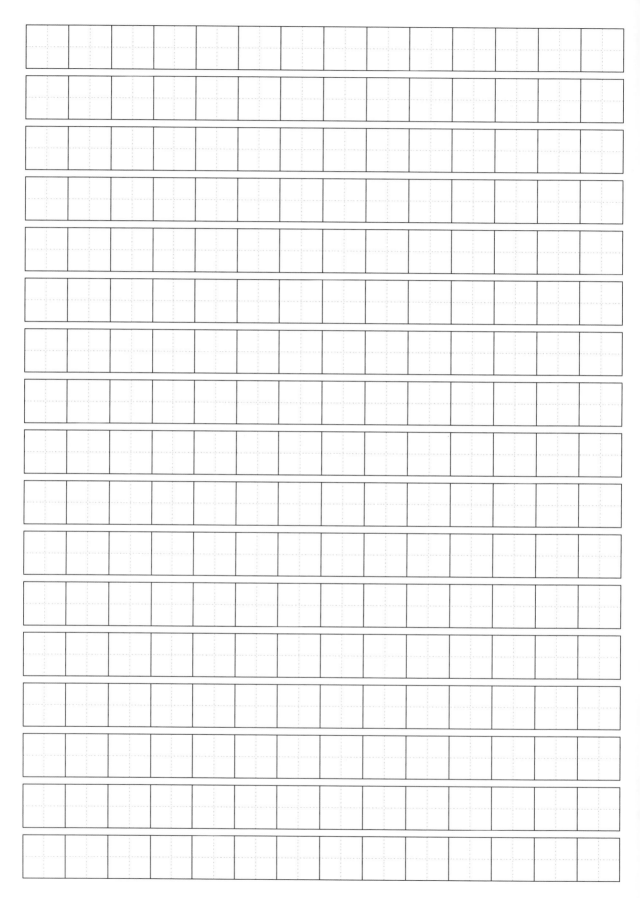

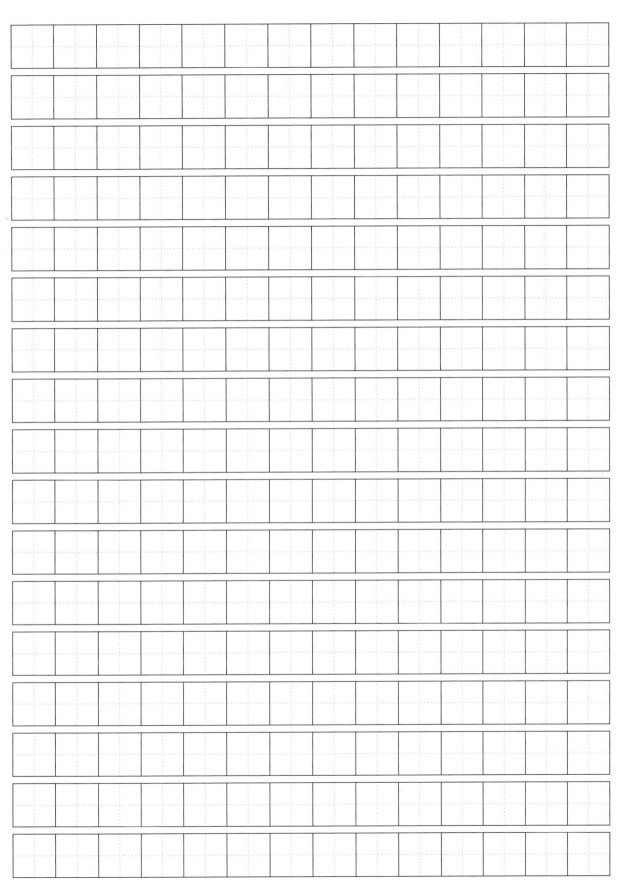

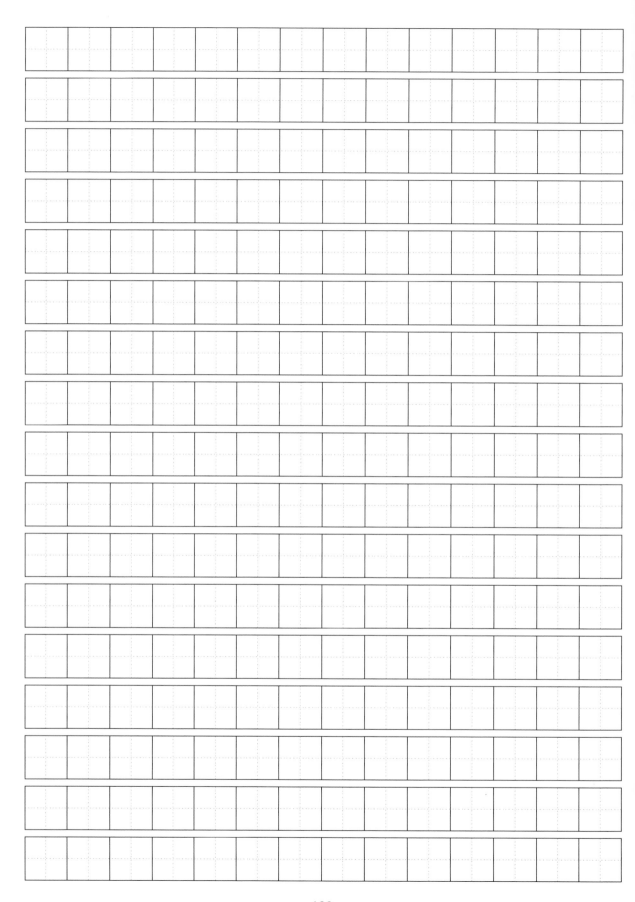

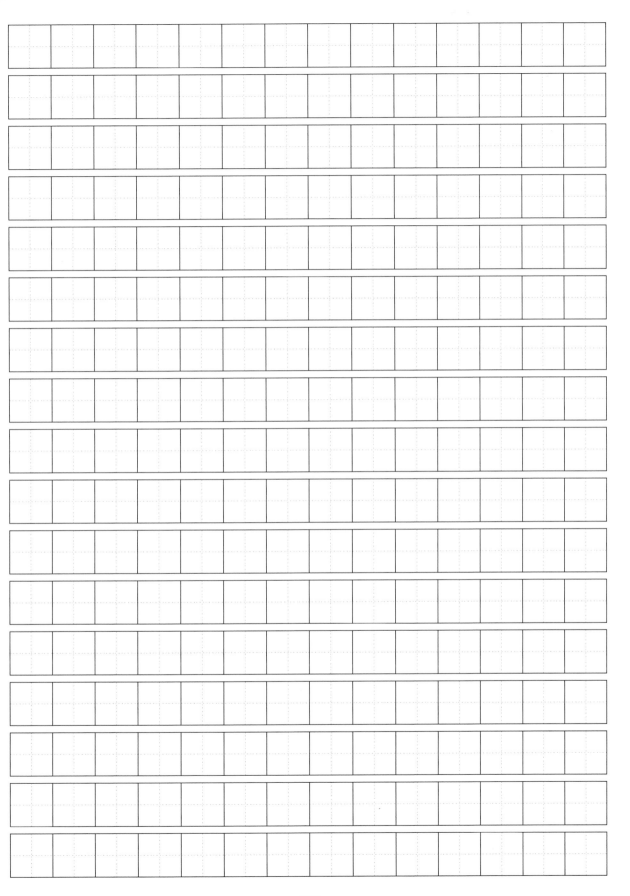

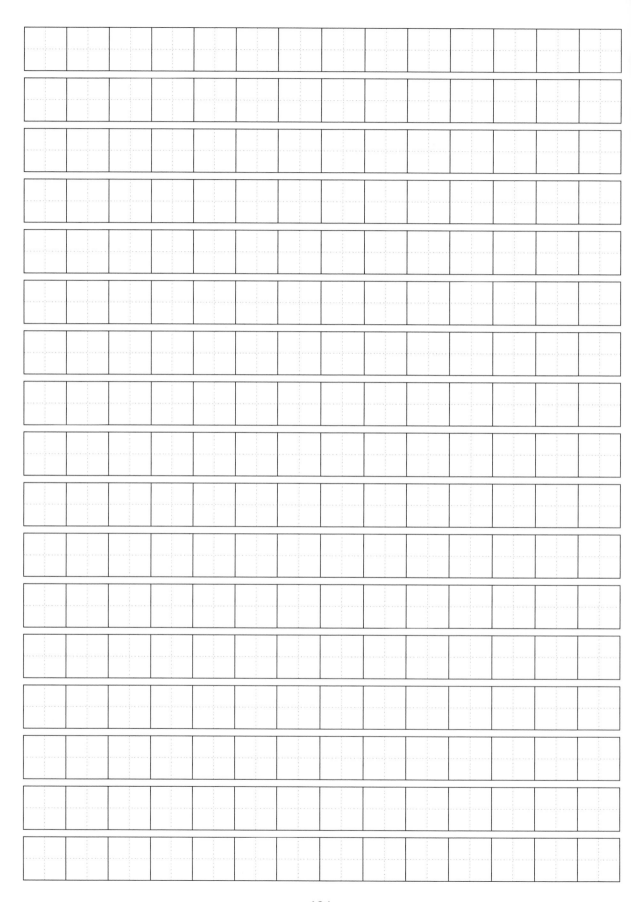

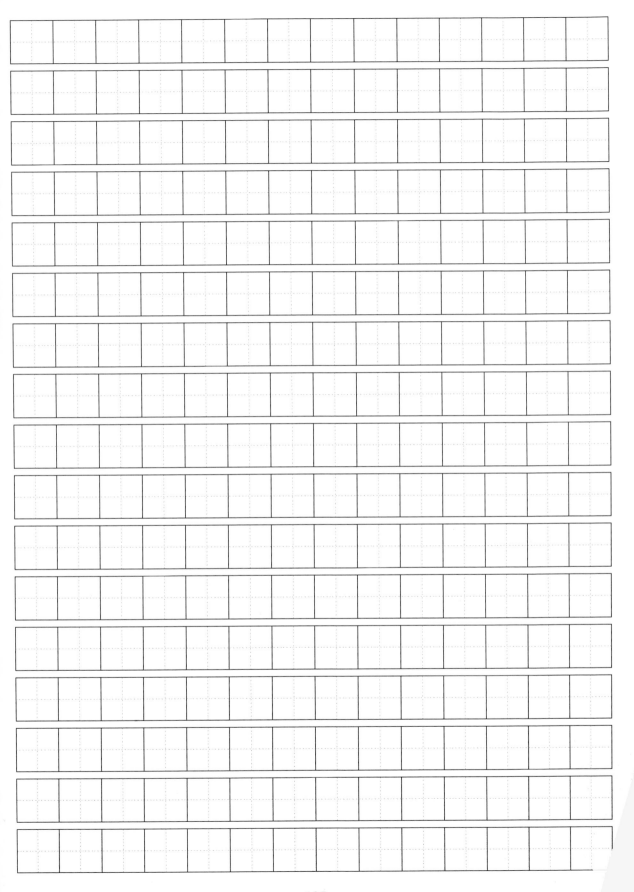

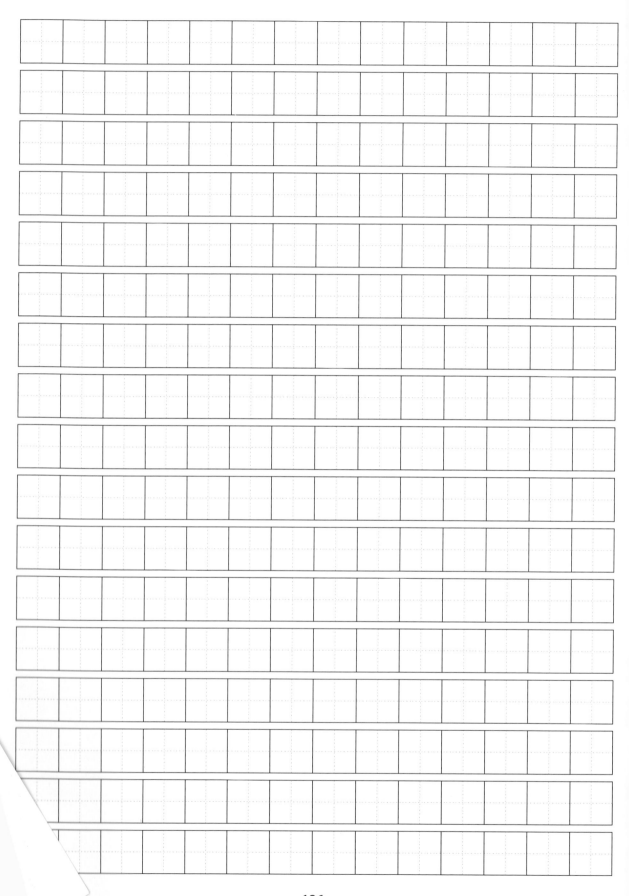

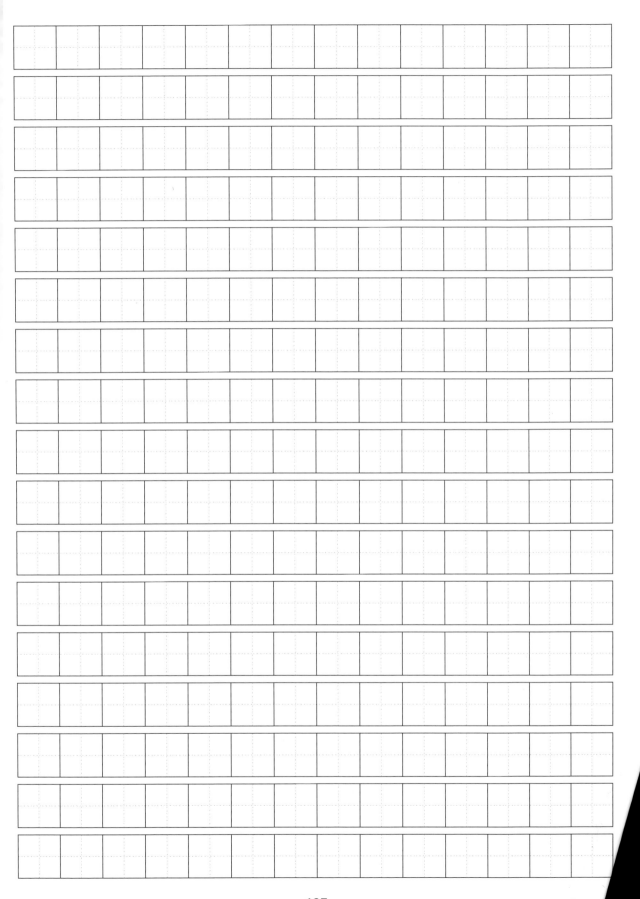

## "Books to Span the East and West"

**Tuttle Publishing** was founded in 1832 in the small New England town of Rutland, Vermont [USA]. Our core values remain as strong today as they were then—to publish best-in-class books which bring people together one page at a time. In 1948, we established a publishing outpost in Japan—and Tuttle is now a leader in publishing English-language books about the arts, languages and cultures of Asia. The world has become a much smaller place today and Asia's economic and cultural influence has grown. Yet the need for meaningful dialogue and information about this diverse region has never been greater. Over the past seven decades, Tuttle has published thousands of books on subjects ranging from martial arts and paper crafts to language learning and literature—and our talented authors, illustrators, designers and photographers have won many prestigious awards. We welcome you to explore the wealth of information available on Asia at www.tuttlepublishing.com.

Published by Tuttle Publishing, an imprint of Periplus Editions (HK) Ltd.

**www.tuttlepublishing.com**

Copyright © 2023 by Periplus Editions (HK) Ltd

Library of Congress Cataloging-in-Publication Data

ISBN 978-4-8053-1740-2

26 25 24 23
10 9 8 7 6 5 4 3 2 1    2304MP

Printed in Singapore

TUTTLE PUBLISHING® is a registered trademark of Tuttle Publishing, a division of Periplus Editions (HK) Ltd.

Distributed by

**North America, Latin America & Europe**
Tuttle Publishing
364 Innovation Drive
North Clarendon, VT 05759-9436 U.S.A.
Tel: 1 (802) 773-8930
Fax: 1 (802) 773-6993
info@tuttlepublishing.com
www.tuttlepublishing.com

**Japan**
Tuttle Publishing
Yaekari Building 3rd Floor, 5-4-12 Osaki
Shinagawa-ku, Tokyo 141-0032
Tel: (81) 3 5437-0171
Fax: (81) 3 5437-0755
sales@tuttle.co.jp
www.tuttle.co.jp

**Asia Pacific**
Berkeley Books Pte. Ltd.
3 Kallang Sector #04-01, Singapore 349278
Tel: (65) 6741 2178
Fax: (65) 6741 2179
inquiries@periplus.com.sg
www.tuttlepublishing.com